the way I see it

the way I see it

an autobiography by
Fr Des Wilson

First published 2005
by
Beyond the Pale
BTP Publications Ltd
Unit 2.1.2 Conway Mill
5-7 Conway Street
Belfast BT13 2DE

Tel: +44 (0)28 90 438630
Fax: +44 (0)28 90 439707
E-mail: office@btpale.com
Website: http://www.btpale.com

British Library Cataloguing-in-Publication Data.
A catalogue record for this book is available from the British Library.

ISBN 1-900960-28-1

Contents

Foreword   vii

1.   Deciding to Change the World   1

2.   From Maynooth to the Mater   21

3.   Teaching Religion   35

4.   The Rights and Wrongs of Sex   41

5.   The Challenge of Christian Unity   46

6.   Appointment of Bishop Philbin   50

7.   Blessed are the Poor   62

8.   Death of the Sixties' Hopes   75

9.   For or Against the People?   91

10. Interval with Soldiers   98

11. Goodbye Sisters   108

12. Problems with the Management   113

13. Peace without Pacifism and Pacifism without Peace   129

14. The McBride Principles   142

15. From Ballymurphy to Boston   148

16. Conway Mill   159

17. Learning the Lessons   161

18. Way Out   173

Appendix I and II   177

Foreword

In 1945 four of us got our Bachelor of Arts degrees at Queen's and headed for the theological College of Maynooth in County Kildare, each with a trunk full of blankets, the rest of our belongings in tea-chests. Going through the big gates of the College we heard a sound which remains with me ever since, the cawing of rooks as they dipped and settled and fought and fled in and out of the great trees at the entrance. Everything about the place is impressive but the Fitzgerald castle at the gates did not attract our attention at the time or the Protestant church inside the Maynooth College grounds or the great mass of Carton House and estate which we passed on our way in and would explore some other time. We went nervously and quietly past the man at the College gate who was affectionately known as Cerberus; what else could he be called in a College steeped in classical Greek and Roman traditions? We were assigned rooms, my Belfast companion and I getting a great high-ceilinged room not far from the entrance with an enormous window which could not be closed properly and through which the ivy clawed its way in the summer and blasts of cold air attacked us in the winter. We were going to be priests.

My companion Johnnie and myself spent a lot of time on and off hauling together on a rope which should have closed the enormous window but didn't; we were like sailors in a storm. Our water supply was outside, arriving through a pump like you would see in a village square, which froze or presented you with near freezing water in the winter, water you collected in a jug which overnight in the room might grow a layer of ice. Without indoor plumbing we had basin, jug and what was known as a Charlie. The toilets, or Johns as they were patiently rather than affectionately called, were about a hundred yards away through open air and sometimes a fog which came rolling in from the surrounding low ground. We had been given one of the few rooms with such primitive conditions; most of the others in the College had running water, but space was scarce even in that enormous college, so many students wanted to be priests, more than sixty in our year alone. Our quarters were known, reasonably affectionately, as Pigs. Primitive as they were, they were only one remove from St Malachy's College in Belfast where we had studied and conditions, if not Spartan, were nothing the Spartans would have been ashamed of.

In Maynooth there was a treat in store when in spring and summer St Joseph's Square and the great grounds would awaken and blossom with smooth lawns dissected by broad paths, thousands of flowers and open playing fields. But going in for the first time in the autumn, while spiritually exciting, was physically and emotionally trying. We went in search of our fellow students from Down and Connor diocese who were there already and so our four years stint in Maynooth began.

I cannot remember anyone in authority actually saying we were welcome. Maybe somebody did but it must have been a rather muted welcome otherwise I would remember it. And we would all have been glad of it.

What I do remember is our first spiritual retreat which began a few days after we arrived. One of the preachers, Fr Cleary, was a stout jolly looking Vincentian, the other, Fr Travers, a thin, sombre looking Vincentian; both were spiritual directors to the College – Travs and Old Tom Cleary, as they were known by the students. Like students in any place with stringent rules, Maynooth students lightened the atmosphere by giving a nickname to nearly everybody on the staff. The President, a formidable scripture scholar, was Shak, for some reason I never knew. One of the deans was, unimaginatively and because his name was Montague, called The Mont. Big Bill, who years later became Cardinal Conway, and others with more or less exotic nicknames would appear to us as time went on but for the moment during the first three-day retreat Cleary and Travers held our almost exclusive attention.

I do not think Cleary welcomed us in his first sermon, but he did say the big gates were open and if we wanted to leave we could do so at any time. Since we had only just arrived and had little opportunity to weigh up either ourselves or the place we had arrived in this seemed a bit premature, and anyway our weighing up the place and finding it wanting was not the reason he gave for our possible departure through the ever-open gates. He laid down such a standard of what our past lives should have been that I began to wonder how the people already here had managed to live up to it. But they must have done, otherwise they would not be here. What virtuous lives they must have led! He went on and on. As I listened to his sermon I had a vision not of a great future opening out before my willing soul but of great white iron gates which were always open not just to receive those who came in but to bid a hearty farewell to those who left. After that opening retreat sermon I was feeling the way the young man in the Gospel must have felt as he walked away sorrowing. The stakes were high but the entrance fee was too high.

Walking round the great square I thought, 'Well, if that is the standard they need here, I'm afraid I'm not in that league'. If I had been around when Christ challenged bystanders to fire the first stone only if they had never sinned, I would have been one of the ones who quietly slipped away. I knew when I was beaten, even though we were just into round one. So I decided to go and find old Cleary and tell him I thought I should reconsider my vocation.

It was one of those silent retreats and being new boys, none of us wanted to break the contemplative silence. I did not, could not, ask anybody where the good Father Cleary's room was, so I could not go and talk to him. I wandered around here and there, vaguely remembered instructions about the layout of the College swirling round in my head, every one of them proving a dead end.

Eventually, as it was getting darker, I decided that since Cleary's verdict on my past life could hardly require that I should leave before midnight, I said whatever prayers seemed relevant and went to bed. I would try again in the morning.

In the morning I woke up wondering what on earth the fuss had been about. That man was asking for an impossible dream. Nobody could be as good as that unless Ireland was once again the island of saints and scholars. So I decided not to go asking him after all and stayed. Later I was to learn one of the richest phrases coined by clerics when faced with impossible demands from liturgists, canon lawyers, preachers or bishops, 'Arrah, don't mind him'. Those wonderful words must have saved many a priest from nervous breakdown and defeat. I have remembered them with relief and gratitude many times since.

Eventually I realised that the big question was not, 'Will I stay?' It was, 'What brought me here in the first place?'

1

Deciding to Change the World

On July the eighth 1925 the Belfast City Fathers were talking about bringing in prohibition 'because it had been so good for the Americans', tenders were being invited to build a new bridge over the railway at Tate's Avenue, Cardinal Logue's will was published leaving his knives, forks and paintings to his successor, Mr. Moncrief was fined ten shillings for driving at 25 miles an hour in a ten miles an hour area and I was born in the Antrim House nursing home on the Cliftonville Road.

Some might say that to be born in Belfast was a misfortune and to stay in it folly, but that is not true. Belfast is full of interesting questions and mystifying answers and good people, so I stayed there for the rest of my life. Its setting in the Lagan Valley is beautiful, the surrounding hills a delight.

My mother came from Saval, near Newry, County Down and all her life believed country people, as she called them, were responsible for everything good in Belfast. She was probably right. The beauty of Saval was enhanced by its people whereas Belfast's beauty was always under threat from some of its people intent on destroying it. City people can destroy in a couple of commercial years what country people have nurtured for a millennium. She often told us, even when we were middle aged adults, that in comparison with the people of County Down Belfast people were not very good. County Down potatoes were praised in the same way.

My father was from County Cavan, making our family true Ulster folk, more so than many people who won prestige, position and money proclaiming their Ulsterhood although they had come from Scotland or England to do it. He wanted to be a teacher and could have been, but just on the verge of being selected as a monitor, the

1

first step towards teacher training in his day, he was displaced by a girl who just happened to be the local canon's niece. He never told me that story. I heard it years after his death. His healthy independence was often frustrated but he had no vindictiveness when it was.

When he came to Belfast at the beginning of the twentieth century, one of the few occupations open to a Catholic man from the country was work in bars. So the licensed trade became well stocked with Catholics. They and their successors laid the foundations of the tourist and hospitality trades, local industries among the few which obstinately refused to be destroyed by political ineptitude. He graduated from bar assistant and union man to co-owner, to owner, Chairman of the Licensed Vintners and with my mother whom he had married in 1916, from a flat in their Chichester Street premises to a house in Rosetta Park in south Belfast and then to another in Knockbreda Park nearby where I spent most of my young years. They left that house in Knockbreda only when they died, my father at 59, my mother at 85. My grandfather lived to be a hundred and two and was outlived by my father by only a short while.

I never knew and never asked why my parents called me Desmond, the only member of their family of five sons – I was the youngest – to be named after a piece of land. The others had family names – James and Liam – or names reflecting our parents' piety – Gerard and Kevin. I was presented at the baptismal font in St. Malachy's church with the request to be called after, not a saint, but a piece of territory in the south of the island, Deas Mumhan, Desmond, South Munster.

The priest was unwilling. There was no saint called Desmond, not yet anyway, and church custom at the time was that children should be given only saints' names at baptism and confirmation. In later years, when church hierarchies were not so strong and people were stronger, many children got names at our baptisms which had little to do with saints and a lot to do with people or things most admired by their parents. In my baby days a child was whisked away to be baptised as soon as possible after birth and so my mother was in no fit state to attend and protest as the priest on his own authority christened me Francis Desmond. So although afterwards I usually got called 'Desmond', or variations of it, the two names 'Francis Desmond' appeared on official documents, the front leaves of schoolbooks and various registers until I got sick of 'Francis' and the bureaucracy which gave him to me and abandoned him.

We never knew whether that Francis was the gentle saint of Assisi, which would have been nice, or the relative of the poisoning Borgias, which would have been regrettable, or Francis de Sales, which would have been very trying because he was a saint of overpoweringly sweet piety and a tendency to explain spirituality in terms of birds and bees. Once I dropped the name it did not matter any more but I hope it was the Assisi saint; after all, he was one of many Christians done down by his fellow Christians and therefore worthy of being encouraged if only for a few years.

Our parents and their young family were fortunate, being able to move fairly quickly out to the suburbs from the centre of the city which was then beginning its slow movement from a sluggish provincial town to the overcrowded, fussy city it was to become. In two moves they were on the city's edge, within short walking distance of fields where we could see and sometimes touch the cows which gave us the sweet and butter milk Paddy Welsh the milkman used to bring in great canisters around our doors by horse and cart. It was a good upward move socially, and historically it meant moving from a street named after a pirate – Chichester – to a park named after St Brigid – Knockbreda. We did not of course realise as children how many of our Belfast streets were named after pirates and adventurers whom our parents would not have allowed us to walk home with if they were still alive.

In early mornings as a growing child I could hear the robin song I never forgot and the sound of great herds of cattle and sheep being driven down the Ormeau Road; we were safe in bed fifty yards away from the nearest of them. They left a mess on the Ormeau Road, but a more healthy mess than the carbon monoxide machines which decade by decade ousted them from the road. Carts painted orange and blue, with great wheels, rumbling downtown from outlying County Down farms bounced and rattled to the markets area where some of our relatives lived and worked. My uncle James, my mother's brother, lived and worked there where the Bull Tavern and the Bakers' Arms and other well named premises defined the area with its bakeries and cattle yards and fresh food markets. For us children, all that was part of a world we thought would never change.

Like other parents of the nineteen twenties and thirties, ours wanted us to be well educated, partly because education was the way to a good position in life and partly because education was a good thing in itself. My mother and my father, who had taken his job in Belfast because he had been diverted from the teaching he really wanted, were both great readers, and I am still not sure whether I learned to read at school or at home from parents and from Cissy, the lady who helped my mother with her housework. I probably learned it at home where these three adults would settle down at a cosy fire with a paper or book and wish for nothing better. The book might be Labour in Irish History, the papers might be the Anglo-Celt for my da, the Frontier Sentinel for my ma and Home Chat or Ireland's Own for Cissy.

Among the men who came into Belfast from Cavan and other counties, there were many who also believed in education for its own sake. They formed debating societies, made speeches and debated politics or whatever happened to be debatable at the time. They went for walks together and talked about politics. They talked interminably about politics, not with the anger which was often their only weapon against inept or cruel politicians but with a compulsive desire to know what their history meant and what those who had created it had really done to them. Walks in the suburbs were for political discourse, the debating societies for literary excitement. My father always kept a tiny dictionary in his waistcoat pocket. He loved making speeches, a love he never succeeded in passing on to any of us. For four of us brothers speeches were a chore to avoid; for me they were a means to an end and nearly always a cause of worry, never of enjoyment. He used to get great delight the morning after a meeting, standing reading to us from the Irish News: 'Mr. Wilson said...' Sadly we did not appreciate him enough at the time, although we did appreciate that to be mentioned in the paper in those days was only for important people; it took decades after that for them to include the doings of what they considered 'ordinary people'.

Our primary school was Rosario, called after our Holy Rosary parish. Boys usually began their schooling with a term or two in the girls' school, an experience I was spared, being sent to school only at six, which was very enlightened, there being enough things to be learned at home without having to submit to the drill of a school. The school, which we ironically referred to as 'the academy', was in Sunnyside Street, girls' school next to boys', founded in 1912; when we were there in the twenties and thirties we did not realise what a modern building it was. The boys' school had three rooms, one presided over by the headmaster, another by an assistant male teacher, another by a lady teacher who had charge of the youngest and obviously most frustrating of the pupils.

I don't believe pupils left that school without being able to read or write, apart from the little lad in the red jersey and shorts who could not speak and was treated with such courtesy by the teachers and the other pupils. I remember senior boys standing in a semi-circle being asked to read out loud, and no-one being shown up or shamed as being unable to do it. Many years later it was surprising that with improved pay, conditions, buildings, methods and all kinds of educational theories as many as one third of pupils were leaving some city schools with very low standards of literacy. It is easy to look through rose-tinted glasses at what the old schools managed to do, but impossible to forget that semi-circle of boys in a primary school reading aloud when called upon and writing compositions which were there for everyone to see.

We were expected to learn and recite some of the most ghastly poems ever invented to satisfy the romantic posturings of precious poets. When I think now of how wonderful it would be to renew the education system from top to bottom I particularly remember that semi-circle of Rosario boys in the depressed nineteen thirties when unemployment and hunger brought ghosts into every street, reciting, 'I wandered lonely as a cloud ... when all at once I spied a crowd, a host of golden daffodils'.

The headmaster, a brilliant man whose talents were uncomfortably restricted by the system, often showed he understood our difficulty by getting the boys to put on fancy accents as they recited that piece, thus providing amusement for us and putting the romantic poets exactly where they belonged. At hymn practice he jazzed up the hymns as he moved hands, feet and elbows at the harmonium to show how a little syncopation could improve our rendering of 'Hail Glorious Saint Patrick'. When I hear 'Toreador' from Carmen I think of Mr. Turley's rich voice resounding around the classroom giving us our first taste of opera. The desks in his classroom were arranged in horseshoe shape so that without warning he could suddenly give up teaching and prance about reciting his favourite nonsense rhyme: 'As I sat on my

Tumpel-teery looking out of my Wumple-weery...'

But every genius has some weaknesses. One of his was that he was too impatient to wait while one of the boys ran out to the yard to soak the cloth for cleaning the blackboard and Mr Turley would spit on the board instead. He would also in times of need spit in the corner which made us like him less than if he had not.

The assistant male teacher who wore plus fours but did not play golf was in love with an assistant lady teacher in the adjoining girls' school but she went and became a nun. The lady teacher of the boys' infants had no love affairs that we knew about. My mental picture of the headmaster, apart from the spit and the 'Toreador' and his sorties into the yard to catch fleeing youngsters who had thrown their school bags out of the windows before getting permission to 'leave the room' and heading for the fields, is of a big man in a blue suit, chalk infested, in earnest conversation with the assistant in plus fours whom we liked to see at other times standing combing his moustache, his back to the radiators or with the infants teacher who seemed never to get chalk on her dark brown velvet dress.

The parish priest who was manager of the school would come in with his great Irish wolfhound, bigger than any of the pupils, and do harmless things like asking harmless questions and go away again.

After about five years at 'the academy', it was time to go on to second level education. We were fortunate to be able even to think of such a thing because for most children schooling ended at primary level. They thought at home I should go to St Malachy's College; all the others in the family did, but the education in Rosario they thought was somehow not good enough to get me in. It was good enough and while the preparatory department of the College was fine, it was not strictly necessary because the primary education we got was better than a lot of people gave it credit for.

Whoever wanted to go beyond primary schooling could do an entrance exam to the College and maybe get a scholarship to pay for the first year or two. They had a helpful system by which through the years of second level schooling at the College the bursar would present every pupil with a bill for tuition and books. He went round the College classrooms giving out the bills but only the bursar knew who actually paid them. The system was the same when some students went on to be priests and lodged in the College. Everyone got a bill and again nobody except the bursar knew who paid it. So it is hard to understand how people can say Catholic diocesan priests can only come from the well-to-do. Some do, some do not. Students could go through from second level to ordination without paying anything, and nobody would be any the wiser. We grew up with the idea that education should be open to everybody. Maybe some time we will look again, with great respect this time, at the education so many of our people managed to get, and give, when there was so little money to pay for it.

In 1935 my father brought us downtown to see the barricades separating the Catholics from the Protestants in some Belfast streets. I thought I knew the reason for them. My father was a broadminded man and he and my mother admired Joe Devlin and De Valera. They were greatly pleased when De Valera won the election in the south in 1932. At times my father had to deal with people like Sir Dawson Bates on behalf of traders. This would have tried the patience of anybody who had sensitivity and intelligence but he seemed to take it in his stride. He seemed to have come to terms with the inevitable humbug in church and state and looked with amused tolerance on the Orangemen, to whose association politicians and judges and other prominent people had to belong.

He would stop the car – we were among the relatively few who had one – and say, 'We'll watch the Brethren' when he heard the sound of Orangemen on one of their thousands of marches. He liked to sit there watching them go by, so we all sat and watched. He knew Orangemen personally and collectively, told how they came around every summer collecting for the Orange Arch which was always the same one as last year, the money being a subscription to no one knew what. He knew that many of them were good in a simple way, and others humbugs. A friend of his, Harry McDonald, was different and had vowed an unending campaign to 'go out for the hypocrite'. 'I'll go out for the hypocrite', he used to intone to my father and he in turn would regale us with their conversation when he came home. Harry had plenty of targets for his ambitious war against hypocrisy because Belfast had more than a fair share of it.

The barricades my father brought us down to see were one of the measures set up by government against the inter-community strife the government itself had created, a measure to be reborn in the nineteen seventies as the 'peace lines' when government was slowly coming round at last to believe that communal peace might suit its purposes better than communal strife. The barricades and the peace lines were both futile as long as the real problem of corrupt government was ignored or encouraged. In family gatherings between my father and mother and my mother's brother, our uncle James, James would describe how Craigavon, a lazy man, had sent telegrams to his followers in Ireland from one of his many trips abroad declaring, 'Well done, big yard, well done, wee yard', a tribute not to the shipbuilding efficiency of the yards but to their success in keeping out the Catholics. Prime Minister Craigavon could go away for months on long cruises in those times without anybody being the wiser or the richer for it and the Archbishop of Armagh could go to Australia with hardly anybody noticing he was gone either. The most important thing in people's minds in the hungry twenties and thirties was their own survival, and the journeyings of the mighty seemed not to have much to do with it.

Governments led us to believe our problems resulted from our people not being able to live together in peace. We did not realise as children – and even for some years to come – that riots broke out on the Belfast streets not because Catholics and Protestants could not live together in peace but because they managed to do it so successfully that the government and its agents had to break them apart again at all costs when they did. Catholics and Protestants successfully living in peace together was against government policy, not against the wishes of the people.

In 1935 the Irish News was delivered every morning at our door and we might read a single line on top of page one like, 'Man shot in Belfast, see page 5'. Newspapers put their news on the front page only years afterwards. In hungry 1932 when there were riots and disturbances all over the world, Belfast Catholics and Protestants came together on the streets to oppose government policies. They had to be separated for the government's sake, so out came the preaching demagogues who told the Protestants that the Catholics were socialist republicans and to have nothing to do with them except destroy them. The friendly cooperation of 1932 soured into the riots of 1935. So the barricades we saw as children were forerunners of the peace lines we would see as adults in the seventies, monuments to London's policy of disrupting poor communities, a policy which never changed. In the nineteen sixties we would see the same pattern emerging, Catholics and Protestants coming together in peace only to be forcibly separated when the time was ripe for it, but this time we were less naive and knew more about what it really meant. In the nineteen sixties people in Belfast showed their desire to live in peace more than at any other time in my life. So as they drew nearer to each other the demagogues came out again.

For every period of peace in the north of Ireland there was always a Paisley and for every Paisley there was always a host of small farmers, small shopkeepers, lodge members, preachers and rich cynics to make sure that the temporary alliance of Catholics and Protestants for a better life would not only fall apart but would be made impossible for years to come. In some countries those who destroy the people's peace are marginalised and curbed; in Belfast they put up monuments to them: Roaring Hanna round one corner, Queen Victoria round another, Carson here, the Black Man there, memorials not to human achievements but to the destruction of humans.

My father and mother, who knew about these things, said little about them. They said little about the death squads of the twenties, about the fear and destructiveness of government and its institutions. They did not want their children to know and have to relive what they and their neighbours had seen and suffered. So when the same happened in our own lives and especially from the sixties on, young people who had grown up not knowing what had happened to their parents wondered why it should be happening to them. For the young ones of the year 2000 the events of the nineteen sixties and the thirty years war after them seemed as remote as the Boer War was to us when our fathers and uncles talked about that.

My parents liked music, and must have enjoyed the variety and music hall that Belfast for all its dourness managed to provide, or at least to accommodate when someone else provided it. Father even half-liked to hear us lazily play the piano badly and would ask, 'Where is the use having piano lessons if you can't play "Ó Donnell Abu"?' He could not sing but tried to sing like Harry Lauder and watched and listened with fascination as the Brethren marched past playing their tunes, some of them his customers and friends – ' That name of mine, Billy Wilson, is worth a thousand a year' – while we would watch and listen indifferently, with no effect for me other than a growing and long lasting distaste for the music of the flute. Only when James Galway came along could I rid myself of it.

In those days in Belfast the Catholic middle class were very conscious of their position and their need to improve it within the system. They were proud of the success of Catholic doctors, lawyers, teachers, politicians, business people. They were pleased with church hierarchies, often speaking proudly about this monsignor or that church administrator. They thought it useful and right for Catholics to be members of the Stormont Commons and Senate, useful ornamental personages who showed that what anyone could do Catholics could do as well and even better. That was a time when the English Catholic paper The Universe would announce with pride that this person who played football for England was a Catholic, or that scientist or whatever. Much of the social life of the middle class Catholics in Belfast was modelled on the big house. When funds had to be raised for a church there were garden parties, ladies even held 'at homes', as well as the more ordinary sales of work and dances. The fashions and language of the big house were adopted by people who needed to express their dignity this way because the society they lived in idolised such things. But the church was a centre and pivot of life for Catholics of all classes. The Catholics were able to put up a better religious show than anybody else in town: music, ritual, words which we had inherited through the centuries, the noises and smells of worship, the lilies, the church missions to which women would go an hour early to get a good seat and the men would follow next week at their leisure.

The mission preachers had to be careful though when talking about sex. In our South Belfast parish a missioner – preaching to people who had little need of threat and great need of encouragement – said that one day parents might experience the horror of having a daughter coming home to announce that she was to 'introduce a bastard into the house'. The effect was electric, but not the way the preacher had hoped. People were shocked; they complained, they mobilised. The local Catholic Senator led a deputation to the parish priest to complain and the preacher apologised next evening, graciously and quietly. No one said the real insult was to single mothers and their children by using words which should never have been used, and none foresaw the day when social customs would change and the meaning of 'respectability' would change with them and all such things would be freely done by many Catholics and talked about even by the children.

In Catholic areas in Belfast the annual Eucharistic processions were long and strong. Our family went to the Eucharistic Congress in Dublin in 1932. I did not know what we were about but our elders did. For the first time in Ireland's history Irish Catholicism was able to express itself in terms and in places of its own choice and it did it with all the splendour that nearly 2000 years had taught it. In Belfast we were still in a state of siege, trying to show we were as good as anyone else; in other places in Ireland Catholics were suggesting they might even be better.

Of Belfast's four parts, north, south, east and west, three died on Sundays. As a priest in 1966 I was going to be pleasantly surprised to find West Belfast stayed uniquely alive and even took on a new lease of life on Sundays. But growing up in the south side we did not ride bicycles on a Sunday in case we offended the religious sensibilities of our neighbours, most of whom were Protestants – what kind of Protestants we did not know or mind. The fundamentalist preacher Professor Savory lived near the top of Knockbreda Park and there were comparatively easy-going Protestants living on each side of us. One thing they had in common was that they all died on Sundays.

Or appeared to die. Our district was so mixed, and there were many like it in Belfast, that it is hard for me to understand why so many people say they never met a Protestant until they went to work or the university, or fell in love or something like that. We met Protestants every day and indeed living in Belfast, unless you were a hermit, you could not miss them. You might not work with them – the religious-political lodges were too influential in giving out jobs for everyone to have that experience; you might not play with them every day, because you did not like soccer or cricket or because they or you liked something else. But they were there and we were there and the twain often met one way or another. We recognised differences, we had to, most of the time not bothering about them too much. We often had to run the gauntlet of pupils of the local Protestant primary school as we walked, or on those occasions ran, to Rosario school. They seemed to believe they had as much right to bait Catholics as the Nazis had to bait the Jews. Growing up like that, playing football and cards and going to the beach often with whoever happened to be around, it was difficult at times to understand why people went on about wanting to know what religion you were. We knew from seeing people going to church, or not going to church, or from their names or maybe from the names on their gates; if a gate carried the name, as the house next door to us did for years, Paray le Monial, you would assume the inhabitants were Catholics. You might even see a holy statue through a window or a picture of a royal William or Elizabeth through a window. But once having learned people's religion, if you wanted to, it did not matter much. We went to different churches or none, we joined different associations or none, we went about our business and if we liked people we liked them; if we did not, then why bother with them? You did not have to like people because they were Catholics or dislike them because they were something else. When as youngsters we bought our first football and went to play in the open fields a few hundred yards from our house, the man in charge of the fields chased the whole lot of us anyway and we were good or bad at the football and the cows left their mess exactly where we would fall on it anyway whether we were Catholics or Protestants And the Ulster Works team who played there too did not want any of us.

The man who came playing a trumpet once a week used to start at the top of the Park and play airs appropriate to the residents, loyal airs for the professor, Irish airs for the family living three doors down, one of whom had been in prison for six months for 'wearing the Easter lily of the republic', airs of general interest while passing other doors, the recital ending at Nazareth House on the Ormeau Road where the trumpeter would get bread and butter and tea from the nuns. We never knew whether he was a Catholic or a Protestant; we just knew he was wise, whatever he was. He was one of many people who coloured our lives: the barrel organ man, coalmen shouting from their carts, the paper man, or paper boy as we always called him although he was years older than us, riding his bicycle throwing the Belfast 'Tele' in at us and giving us a free copy of Ireland's Saturday Night while whistling hymns as he rode along. The street musicians did not have to call at house doors; the people came out to them. And every morning in spring and summer you could waken up to the sound of 'sweet sweet sweet sister vee' of a bird whose name I never troubled to discover then but heard again years later with a lot of joy in Donegal summers.

When I was 75 and my brother Gerard a bit older I asked him one day if he knew whether people who lived for years next door to us when we were children were Catholics or Protestants. Like myself, he did not know.

We thought we understood why our district died on Sundays but we were not quite right. The row of houses to the left of ours went in an arc or crescent and on Sundays the road in front of those houses was empty: no bicycles, no noises, no whistling Catholics. It was only after some years we realised that our delicacy on Sundays was misplaced. When we were all making our own living and mother was getting a bit older, we got a new window in our kitchen and this gave us what we did not have before, a view of the backs of the houses in the crescent. My mother and myself looked out with surprised interest. In back garden after back garden people were washing cars, hanging out washing, doing odd jobs. We then realised that while the house fronts were dead, the backs were very much alive. We had been observing the Sabbath better than our neighbours were!

Whatever benefit or pain Sabbath observance gave to the Protestant neighbours in those days it was a great boon to the Catholics who played golf. There is a superb golf course near the top of the Ormeau Road, Belvoir Park. Every Sunday the eight o'clock Mass in Holy Rosary Church was attended by ardent golfers who at the end of their worship went from the church in dignified haste either by way of home and a quick breakfast or straight to the first tee. The principled but probably unhappy golfers who did not share the Catholic faith with its relaxed ideas of religious duty on Sundays went only as far as the clubhouse, from which they looked out sadly as Catholic after Catholic teed up and went happily down the first fairway. P.G. Wodehouse would have delighted in such a theme of golfers sadly denied and yet courageously holding on to their principles.

Eventually, like all good things, this came to an end because the Sabbath observance became less and less rigid and it began to appear to our neighbours that playing golf on Sunday need not lead to loss of reputation, job or church membership after all. Changing times in Belfast eventually brought advantages for Catholics but for the golfers among them one great disadvantage, that they no longer had Belvoir Park golf course almost to themselves on a Sunday morning.

And like other good things Rosario schooling came to an end too. For second level education I was put into the preparatory department of St Malachy's. Gerry McDermot, the teacher in charge of 'prep', was also gym master and ran a pleasantly easy-going department. While there I began to think what I would like to be. My trouble was that while I possibly had some ability I certainly had a lot of laziness. I liked writing and there were plenty of things to write about – Michael McLaverty and Brian Moore, Bernard McLaverty and many others have shown how successful Malachian writers are – but at school it was adults who decided what was interesting enough to be written about. Only much later did we learn that some of the most interesting things to write about are what adults want to avoid.

We all looked forward to going along the College academic path from Prep into Junior and Senior with little difficulty, because we lazy people always have ways of getting to places we want to go. I had a blockage about maths and when I passed an exam in it I thought the examiners had made a mistake, a mistake I was not going to question. It was a matter of getting into what we thought of as 'good' classes, doing some work, finding useful summaries and passing exams which turned out to be less difficult than we had been led to believe. All went reasonably and undeservedly well. Our student world was divided into people of two kinds, those who were able and wanted to pass as well as they could and those who were very able and just wanted to pass and get on with life. I had sufficient lack of perception to belong to the second of these. Years afterwards I regretted such a waste of opportunities.

And there were so many opportunities. At different times in life we had chances to learn languages, Irish, English, Latin, Greek, Hebrew, French or any other, but so what? Language was often taught by excellent and pure grammarians as if we were all going to become writers or critics of great literature instead of inquisitive travellers who might just want to ask people behind counters and in buses about their world even in ungrammatical terms. Some of the literature offered us in all language departments was enough to put us off literature for years to come. They seemed to pick such boring things for us to read. The Latins and Greeks seemed to us not to have a sense of humour, or their humorous literature was considered improper for us so we did not get it. Horace could raise a smile but not a laugh. And we had to read how Julius Caesar helped slaughter a million of our ancestors in eight years of his Gallic wars. What a sorry task we had understanding them. An even sorrier task trying to like them.

So the educational idea we had then – apart from those

unaffectionately known as 'stews' – was minimalist; you get by. Thus many of us wasted the work – often exasperated work – of some of the best academic minds in Belfast as we reluctantly did our 'eckers', copying from each other only in times of emergency. The definition of emergency varied from student to student. For brilliant teachers it was a trying situation.

Down town in Smithfield there were bookshops selling first hand, second and third hand books, improving books and not at all improving books and most useful of all, translations of Latin and Greek texts. I gave up all efforts to learn Greek in a year of wasted effort by teachers and no efforts of mine. We had to do Latin. Somebody bought a translation of Cicero's speech against Verres which even we admired as a powerful speech with biting invective, crushing irony and fierce condemnation of a great villain. We enjoyed the vitality of it but preferred to read it in English. We would be called on to translate the Latin text in class, having prepared a section of it the previous night. One day a student who did not take any trouble at all whereas most of us took some trouble, just held the translation behind his Latin text and read it. The teacher, J.J. Campbell, listened quietly for a while. Then even he could take it no longer as the class burst out laughing. The student was giving out, as if it were his own translation of Cicero's biting irony against Verres, the phrase, 'And so this paragon of disinterested impartiality...' Even the most tolerant of teachers could hardy let that pass as a student translation, certainly not by one of us. From then on we were more cautious members of the Smithfield School of Ciceronian Translation.

I thought I might be either a scientist or a journalist. I even went to science classes I did not have to go to. But writing and reading were interesting, and there was constant reading at home. As for science, I learned more outside the classroom than in it. I don't understand why people despise what they call street corner learning. Street corner learning is useful, necessary even, and the street corner was a place of learning long before the schools. There was a magazine called Armchair Science in which we learned about amazing things to come. This was in the hungry nineteen thirties and they were writing about jet engines, space travel and even what they called test tube babies. Those of us who read this magazine every fortnight did not understand all of it, and believed only some of it, but Armchair

Science got a lot of things right and we lived to see much of it come true: going to America in few hours in a jet plane, hearing people talk from the moon, while in vitro fertilisation and other predicted things became just small items for the newspapers.

So which would it be? Journalist? Scientist? Becoming a priest did not enter into the picture. I had respect for priests; they were good to me. An elderly priest living near us, who had got into trouble for drinking too much, was a good friend and we often visited him. He said Mass in his own house and we sometimes served it. He was a gentle soul, one of many among the priests, perhaps too sensitive for the kind of world he was in and the kind of life he would be required to live.

Our parish priest was a good soul too, but brusque, whose great Irish wolfhound may have been for his own protection as much as for ornament although we did not think of that at the time. We did not attach much importance to his telling us again and again in his sermons about how we needed to take care of the 'poor little innocent children'. We did not realise how some of them suffered or who was responsible for it. I suppose now that he did.

These were good men but I saw no reason to follow in their footsteps. The idea of journalism or science as a career left my mind only when special circumstances put the idea of priesthood into it. They put it not only into my head but into the heads of other students who were about to leave the College in 1942. The choice of journalism or science had seemed exciting. Years later when most newspapers became enslaved to advertising and circulation, when media empires were built up for maximum profit and standards of reasonable journalism upheld by fewer and fewer journalists who required more and more courage, I was glad I did not become one. The word, the sacred word was surely not meant just to sell merchandise. Strangely though, I did eventually write columns at different times for six different papers: *The Evening Press, The Irish News, The Northern Standard, The Irish People, The Catholic Standard* and *The Andersonstown News*. But that began almost by accident many years later. What changed my mind and the minds of other final year College students was what was happening to us in Belfast. The ten year old child being shown the barricades by his father in 1935 and seeing family members running the gauntlet of schoolboys who might later grow into men and women with power was now nearing sixteen and wondering why the President of the College told the boys they should wear their school uniforms even at the risk of getting attacked in the streets and why one of the boys from his class had got shot in the leg on his way to school. There were things in Belfast that science or literature had not made us wonder about but experience had.

The war came in 1939 and our elders talked about how they had fought against conscription in 1917 and we felt in advance the horror of anyone's father, brothers, friends being led off to fight in a war that had nothing to do with them if a greedy and scruple-free London government needed their bodies. And then the air raids. Watching the crowds of frightened people streaming out of the city, seeing the fires, not knowing that the nearest bomb was a mile and a quarter away from us. Visiting a dancing, singing, friendly family on Saturday night in Gloucester Street and never seeing them again because they were blown to bits on the Tuesday. After one of those air raids I walked across the city to the College past ruins and fire hoses and firefighters and engines with the smell of burning which was to be in my nostrils time after time in later years as Belfast again and again writhed in the pain its bad leaders inflicted on it.

Then my Father died in 1942, the first time our family had experienced death so close to us.

I thought, 'Surely there has to be a better life than this'.

It seemed unlikely that either science or journalism would give it to us. That was science up there in the night sky droning over our heads, that was science blasting our streets and our friends, and there was journalism in the shape of *The Belfast Telegraph* announcing on its placards: 'Ulster's Night of Thrills', as if somebody somewhere was delighted that the Germans had at last recognised us as part of Britain, somebody who lived safely in the countryside.

We thought – we had been taught – that the better life could come through the church, which had the answer to so many problems of what life was about. We believed that if we became priests or members of religious orders that would give us the means to make changes. Some of us in our last year at the College decided to do that.

I went to visit the friend who sat beside me in school to tell him what I had decided to do to change our world. His mother opened the front door of their house opposite Clonard Monastery. I told her. She told me: 'Arthur has decided on the same thing, only he wants to work

abroad'. In the next few days both of us heard of other students who
made decisions of the same kind. The world needed change and we
could help to change it.

It took a long time for us to realise how many problems were born
and nourished inside the churches too, how many problems and
hardships the churches condoned for the sake of gains they believed
important for themselves. And what we thought was their ability to
change the world was at best an ability to help people cope with a
world that was not willing to be changed by anybody.

Our idea then was to leave school as quickly as possible, get into the
university or religious community as soon as possible, follow the
fastest course available, get to Maynooth or some other theological
college, become priests and help change the world. One day I met one
of our Rosario school teachers on his way to church; he stopped me
and asked what I was going to do. I told him. He took the cigarette
from his mouth, looked closely at me and said, 'Do you know in
Maynooth they will ask you to plant cabbages upside down? If they
do, do it'. That, he assured me, was a way of testing your obedience.
I did not heed him because people said strange things about churches
and their methods, many of them untrue. Seven years later, finished
with Maynooth, successfully ordained, I thought I should visit Mickey
and tell him they never asked me to plant anything upside down after
all. But I forgot.

The President of St Malachy's College, Fr. John McMullan was
decent and seemed disorganised; he would stand in the school
corridor at the beginning of term, grasp students by the arm and direct
them, apparently willy nilly, into this class or that. He was a brilliant
teacher of ancient Classics and must have had a plan but as youngsters
of about twelve plus we found ourselves directed into Irish or Latin or
Greek or all three without discussion about our attitude to any of
them. Education was based on Latin and Greek literature, literature
which embodied among other things the thoughts, ideals and images
of the Roman Empire, one of the most wicked empires ever known.
Some of the images of Roman and Greek mythology are of surpassing
foulness. The Latin literature we had to read, or which was censored
so that we could read only parts of it, had examples of ferocity and
crassness that could hardly have done a child anything but harm.
Maybe the educators thought that if we could stand the cruelty of the

Old Testament we could stand anything.

Brought up with that literature, with the Old Testament and with whatever Shakespeare and Milton could throw at us, the students were still remarkably civilised, perhaps because most of us did not take the crudities, the crassness, the cruelties, the sexual obsessions of the literature seriously. But we did not feel willing to spend more time at it then we needed.

When I decided to leave school to go to university, John, or Jakie as we knew him, said I should stay on at school for another year to get a sufficient grounding for Queen's University. Not being interested in an academic career and wanting to get into the university as quickly as possible and out the other end just as quickly, I looked forward to just enough work to get through the hoops in between. For John, the Greek scholar, that must have seemed, to use the word his revered Greek authors used, barbarous. He thought that if I went in without that extra year I might do badly; if I stayed in school for another year I might do really well. I believed if I stayed at school I would probably waste the extra time, knowing I had enough passes to get into Queen's already. John did not insist and my mother did not either – she had a lot else on her mind, a widow looking after a business and a family, all of whom were still studying too – and so I went to Queen's.

One of the recurring dreams I had for many years afterwards was of going into an exam and suddenly realising I did not have to because I had passed it already. Another was of going into an exam and suddenly realising I had read none of the books. There was a bit of truth in both. The fact that exam dreams persisted for so many years shows how our minds got filled with them to the exclusion of the better things of life.

Learning things other people wanted me to learn did not seem interesting enough to keep me at school for a whole unnecessary year; getting through whatever hoops were put up to get to where I wanted to go seemed more reasonable, if not very ambitious.

Church students resided in St Malachy's College while attending Queen's and had a rigorous regime of going to lectures and coming back briskly with little opportunity for savouring the delights of the recreations available in the university. There were not all that many; students' unions seemed to become exciting and interesting only about two decades later.

Lectures were often boring, even if you wanted to be good and study a lot. So boring that some students would throw pennies at the most boring of the lecturers, a cruel and wrong thing to do, and once they brought in a barrel of water setting it on the top steps of a lecture theatre hoping it would topple over during an unexciting lecture about Fanny Burney. It stayed there motionless and next time they brought in a little dog in the hope it would bark during a lecture on Tristram Shandy. The dog went to sleep and this was accepted as a sign that there was no antidote to third level educational boredom and we would have to sit it out.

In the university there were many wasted opportunities too, wasted not only by us but by the people who ran it. It was a good training ground for doctors, lawyers, engineers and so forth but hardly a place for the excitement of sharing ideas or creating them. The university like our other institutions at the time was not afraid of ideas; it was afraid only of fresh ones. Some lecturers repeated the same lectures year after year. None of them had to compete for an audience, or entice us in by their brilliance; you had to attend 45 per cent of lectures or be kept out of exams and so they could be dull if they wanted to. They seemed more keen to research – or at least write research papers – and get published than to teach or explore ideas with students. If we had been keen enough on academic or intellectual study we might have objected to this and asked for change, but most of us were content to get through the hoops. Many years later when a bigger number of mature students were going into universities it became more frustrating if they got little opportunity to exchange ideas and too much information simply in order to recycle it. The lecturers who struggled to give something better became more and more valued, certainly by the mature students.

Anyhow, for good or ill I was allowed to head for the university as soon as the results of the 1942 exams said I could.

And I left with a low grade degree three years later.

2

From Maynooth to the Mater

For four of us, Frank, Finbar, Johnny and myself, the next step on our way to become priests was St Patrick's College, Maynooth, County Kildare. The College is beautiful, with fine buildings and grounds and a history you can argue over. It was set up in 1795 by a British government frightened at the number of young men going to continental Europe for education refused to them at home. The government thought, quite correctly, that they would pick up revolutionary ideas over there. Better have them at home, even if the government had to pay for it. It would not pay for the education of Catholics for many other reasons. When we went there in the nineteen forties it was part of the National University of Ireland. It was also a Pontifical University, that is, it was qualified to give university degrees recognised by authorities in Ireland and religious authorities in Rome. That made it different from Queen's. Another thing that made it different was that somehow, even as we entered the hard gates through Spartan halls and rooms to a tough regime, it seemed more our own. We expected a tough regime; that is the way church training and education in general were at the time; it was tough for everybody and even tougher for student priests. But even a harsh regime always finds some place sooner or later for the gentler urges of humanity. Institutions never completely conquer the human spirit and its latent generosity, so we remained optimistic.

Through our first spiritual retreat and swift induction into the Maynooth way of life we found out about all that. The techniques of the two spiritual directors, Cleary and Travers, would be familiar both to mission-goers in Ireland and to victims of police interrogations, the soft approach followed by the hard one. Big Tom Cleary would be tough in the pulpit, a lamb in private conversation; he the strong preacher, Travs the quiet intellectual. Travs not Tom Cleary would be out playing tennis with the students in the summer.

Never a fervent student, I agreed with the many for whom subjects, studies and exams were hoops to jump through to get where you wanted to go, to be priests and get out there and change the world. We reckoned that what we would have to study in our approach to each hoop would have only limited value later on for us potential world changers. And we realised much later on that we would be blessed indeed if ten years after ordination the world had not drastically changed us. To keep your ideals intact and then use ideals plus experience as a launching pad for fresh ideals and new adventures was more difficult than we had thought. Even to stay where you were spiritually and intellectually instead of moving backwards was a great feat in itself, the world being as it is.

Most of us would not need the Hebrew and the biblical Greek, and in any case, perpetually studying the ideas of other people who were so self-assured that theirs were always best was not going to help us much in Belfast or Larne. The treatises on morality we studied were fine examples of academics having a wonderful time making distinctions and divisions and categories and reckonings of the gravity of sins, but all that would be of little use when talking to someone writhing under the lash of anger, desire, frustration or all three of them. Some of the 'spiritual reading' recommended to us, books by St Francis de Sales for instance, might have appealed to beekeepers and precious thinkers but not so much to those of us whose lives had been and would be spent with the noise of trams and cars and hammers and Orange flutes in our ears. Horses for courses. De Sales and a Kempis were recommending to us a contemplative life far from what we would be getting into after ordination. A priest who would be too busy even to read The Busy Pastors' Guide would be unlikely to turn successfully to either of these writers for strength or guidance. And ecclesiastical libraries including Maynooth were full of such.

Writers like these were presented to us as guides, maybe because there was so little religious writing suited to our way of life. The church seems not to have come to terms with priests living alone in the world and yet playing an active part in it and therefore does not have an adequate literature about them. Maybe it is an impossible ideal anyway. When we felt uneasy about not being able to relate to such 'spiritual reading' we thought this was due to our lack of spiritual sensitivity. But really it was more likely due to our trying to live up to a monastic ideal while living a life the church has never properly understood. A literature to reflect, appreciate and inspire pastoral priests has still to be written. Fortunately the Gospels brought alive for us the simplicity of what we were trying to do. But thinking this way about it came much later.

Maynooth education was like third level education in other places; it tended to be a succession of lectures by academics, some interesting, some boring. At times there was excitement though, like the history lectures by the professor nicknamed John Eck. He was a Donegal O'Doherty. He paced up and down the dais and made history live, bringing welcome reality into our student vision as he described the appalling take-over of the papacy by crooks and the lustful adventures of those who did it. Some lecturers were content to read to us while we wrote notes. Some had a discursive style, like the professor nicknamed Baked Jack; the word 'baked' was put on people whose studies had made them not speechless but confused. Some seemed anxious to get you through exams, some let you know you had better study or appear to study or you would get little sympathy from them. But all of them were probably just as anxious to get us through and on our way as we were. Beneath even the most forbidding of exteriors there was a decent man. None of them treated us as starkly as the professor in Queen's who told us on our first day at his lectures on English Literature, 'You will hear nothing in this lecture theatre which will be of use to you in the examination hall'. Since the aim of most of us was to get through the examination halls unscathed and quickly that was daunting. Students create their own, sometimes eccentric, defences. The student who sat beside me in Queen's calmly chewing liquorice root during those English Literature lectures and who kindly offered me some became a magistrate away down south; another who sat looking around him later became a unionist politician, Orangeman and attorney general and then had his political career ruined by being hauled up before the Presbyterian Assembly in Belfast to get a wigging for failing to protect the Presbyterian Assembly from abuse from Paisley. So of the three of us, one fell out with a Presbyterian Moderator and the other two fell out with two Catholic bishops. So they did not remain bored for ever.

The simplest thing to do in Queen's and Maynooth then was to listen, write, get through exams and get away.

In Maynooth those who took their studies more seriously, won lots of prizes and were known as 'bakes', had different ideas. They loved the studies, however arcane, for their own sake or because they wanted to progress in the church not only heavenwards but possibly palace-wards as well. Ordinary folk for whom winning a prize was a pleasant surprise rather than an expected reward, wanted to move not upwards but sideways in the church. Moving upwards you could easily get out of sight; moving sideways you could bump into unexpectedly interesting people. Maybe some students prayed to be made bishops. One hopes some of them prayed not to be.

There must have been some who would one day say a polite 'thank you but no, thank you' to the Papal Nuncio when he sent them an invitation to be made bishops. Some said you could not refuse. But you could of course refuse. You say 'no' and they will find someone else. The men who say 'yes' to bishoprics may not realise how many problems are waiting for them after they take office.

Of the sixty five in our class ordained on June 19th 1949 four were made bishops. You hear the news of these promotions with mixed feelings. Some priests want to be bishops and it is fine for them and those who are happy with the system. It is disappointing, maybe hurtfully disappointing, for those who want but do not get. But the best work for the church may well be done not by people in positions of power and authority but by those who are free to experiment, people who would not be damaged but would learn something new even when something they try turns out wrong. In the Maynooth of our time the 'bakes' were reckoned to be on their way to becoming bishops, lecturers and lawyers. A good memory was a great asset to them, but unfortunately you could go successfully through universities and seminaries with a good memory even if you had little else. Since you could get through exams with a good memory, those who had one to start with were at an advantage; those who did not have one had to slog it out. But if you can pass exams by a good memory, is it possible you are going out to work with little else? The ability to analyse and discuss and forecast may well be diminished, not improved, by relying on memory so much. You could win prizes. You could become one of the many academics in line for bishoprics. And in the end the church could find itself blessed by a line of bishops whose most developed intellectual quality was memory, with little besides. What will it profit a man if he remembers a whole library and loses his soul, and everybody else's? In time the church could have leaders trying to solve problems by reciting what this chapter of the law said, or what was done at the Council of Trent, or in 1932, or at the Second Vatican Council, when the real question in our minds is not what we did yesterday but what we are going to do today and tomorrow. So we should not become too dependent on academics without deep experience of the world outside their books and institutions. We need experimentation and inventing new things too much for that.

Sometimes priests lamented an episcopal bench consisting mostly of academics. Some shook their heads sadly when yet another of their colleagues accepted a bishopric, possibly one of those friendly, good hearted 'bakes' whose rare and leg flinging incursions on to our student football field had forced the rest of us at exam time to pad our shins, sometimes with wads of photocopied notes on the early Fathers of the Church.

A new bishop often does not know what he is in for because most problems in church are not talked about openly; many are best dealt with privately and quietly anyway. It is a delicate business. When men become bishops and get to know startling things they knew nothing about beforehand they can react in different ways: by avoiding the problems, or by dealing with them so severely that people stop telling them, or ideally by creating a climate of trust and openness to help clergy and others to solve problems rather than expect them to be solved for them. There are all kinds among the Irish bishops. Some crumpled under the strain of unaccustomed problems. Some headed for cover. Some settled for what they could manage and reduced their expectations of themselves. Some were quietly and gracefully successful.

A few tried to push into new territory. Peter Birch, a member of the Maynooth staff when we were there, was one of these. He wanted to be a bishop. He was very visible and helpful to bishops when they visited Maynooth and that helped. But as events showed, his ambition was not for personal glory but because he believed he could make real changes in the church. And he did make them. He exchanged the big house for a small one, set up organisations for welfare and had a lifestyle which separated him from the Byzantine splendour which some bishops thought was their due.

He inspired people, including people in Belfast, much as James McDyer, regenerator of Glencolmcille did. At a cost of course, as he said himself. Some clergy were afraid he was getting separated from them; others believed he was getting nearer to other people in the church, which was a very different thing. Some bishops were uneasy with his reforming programme because people might think all the bishops should be doing the same. Sometimes there was tension between them and him. He joked about how strange it was that his hospital check-up appointments seemed by some strange chance to fall on the same dates as episcopal conferences and so he had to make the choice, conference or hospital. Most times he chose hospital.

The bishops' fear that if one of them did something out of the ordinary, people would ask all of them to do it, was real. A young bishop wanted people to stop calling him 'My Lord' and encouraged them to stop it. At the first bishops' conference he attended he was told gently but effectively that young bishops do not rock episcopal boats, that it was a grand idea but would make things difficult for the others. He went back to his diocese and consented to be called 'My Lord' like most of the rest of them.

Peter Birch did indeed get separated from other bishops and from some of his own clergy while trying to get closer to others, but he did pioneering work and it succeeded. People did not call him a communist like they did to Jimmy McDyer, but in Jimmy's day if people got afraid of change they would call you a communist; later it would be 'Provo priest', as some of my friends and I were called, or fascists. These terms of abuse change according to how effectively abusive they think they are, not according to their real meaning. Tomorrow the terms of abuse will change, but abuse will be hurled for much the same reason, your insisting on unwelcome change.

Another Irish bishop who refused to be ambitious was asked if he was interested in transferring from his small diocese to the larger Down and Connor. He said simply, 'Not at all. If I did, what would become of my fishing?' He appreciated life's real beauties.

Maynooth's theological college has changed greatly in recent years, partly because of enlightened staff, partly because students realised they should be treated differently. When the four of us went to

Maynooth in 1945 we were only on the edge of those changing times and therefore did not reap the benefit, but good luck to those who did.

Many years later, visiting Maynooth after it had opened up as a general university, I paused outside one of the lecture halls. A woman was standing there with a pram and her lovely baby. We greeted each other. No, she said, she was not a visitor. I was the visitor, she was a student. Maynooth had indeed changed right enough.

Of the four men ordained with me who became bishops Kevin McNamara was one of the most obviously brilliant. A constant prize winner in Maynooth he studied incessantly apart from pre-exam times when he would join the sluggards among us on the football field, not to show off sporting skills but, we believed, to clear his head. The 'bakes', too zealous for our comfort and raising the academic standards on the rest of us, were all right in their rooms or the libraries, but on the football field showed a lack of coordination of flailing legs and arms which often dented the limbs of the unwary. Diarmuid O'Sullivan of Kerry, Michael Murphy of Cork and Gerry Brooks of Dromore were less obtrusively academic than Kevin. He was appointed professor in Maynooth soon after ordination and was involved in creating the Maynooth Summer School.

The Summer School seemed a good idea and many of us gladly encouraged it. I was one of those who mistook what it was about, believing it would be an annual refresher course for priests who did not have much opportunity to keep up with what the books were saying, the 'too busy to read The Busy Pastor's Guide' people. Priests who want a theology more adapted and more relevant than what we had had as students. It turned out not quite like that and having attended the first one, and the second one, I stayed away from the rest. When the first one was about to open we were standing talking in the beautiful St Joseph's Square in Maynooth and someone asked, 'By the way, will there be time for questions from the floor after each of these lectures?' Kevin McNamara's answer was swift, sure and revealing. 'Oh, I don't think anybody would really be qualified to ask questions at these lectures.' Our hearts sank. This was going to be no refresher course after all but a concentrated academic performance by high academic performers. Once we had dutifully attended a couple of the Summer Schools we quietly slipped away and were never missed. Our old theology would have to do us and we had to make the best of it.

And we left the 'bakes' to it.

Thirty years after ordination, at a conference in Dublin on torture, British government torture having become a public scandal in the North, something suddenly dawned on me. A lecturer was describing how prisoners had everything taken from them which expressed their personality, ties, personal clothing, then were cut off from the outside world by not having newspapers, or radio, had to wear uniform clothes and were subjected to a strict regime in which they could make few decisions or none. This gave me a start and without thinking I turned to a man sitting beside me and said, 'I had that for four years'. He turned to me with wide eyes. 'You mean you were tortured?' With great embarrassment I excused myself and said I was not thinking, I would explain afterwards. Then I told him about the theological colleges, about the black clothes, the absence of newspapers, the strict regime, the outlawing of 'singularity' or just difference, the oneness. It wasn't torture; it was just the way we thought future priests should be trained. There were many educationalists who believed you could reduce a personality almost to nothing and then remould it according to the book, your book. But even out of Maynooth, one of the strictest of the character moulding institutions, came an astonishing mixture of people. Priests who came out of Maynooth were conservative or liberal, conservative/liberal, hardworking or lazy, amusing, boring, good at it, not good at it, permanent or temporary, but all had been trained in the same rigorist school which tried to make them all the same. A basic principle of that rigorist education, borrowed from old Aristotle, is that if you keep on doing a thing often enough it will become a habit. But this is not necessarily true. The opposite may happen. If you do a thing often enough because you want to it may become a habit; if you do not want to, you reject it as soon as you can, no matter how many times you had to do it. There were Maynooth students who vowed they would never get up at 6.30 in the morning again as long as they lived although, possibly because, they had done it for the most of seven years in Maynooth.

After ordination in 1949 I went to work for a month in Glenravel parish, County Antrim. I was shocked. Not by wickedness revealed to an innocent priest but by the innocence of the people the priest was supposed to guide. My first experience of the confessional box made me detest confessional boxes ever after. This was no clearing house for the sins of the people; it was a place of revelation where, confronted with the goodness of people you could only feel more and more inadequate. What on earth was I doing here with these good people who worked so hard, suffered so much, got so little return for their life's work and as far as the people in high places were concerned were subjects, not fellow citizens of God's kingdom?

Mass and some other religious services, visiting housebound people for the First Friday, doing the few things people demanded while the parish priest was away on his month's holiday, that was all I had to do. He told me I need not do anything else. I think he was afraid I would go doing things the way a brash ex-student would do them, fresh out of the books. Better have a small amount done safely than a lot done with the rashness of which young men of twenty five are capable.

That month in the parish had more effect than a hundred sermons. I had always lived in the city and had more than enough company during seminary days, so a month in the country seemed very lonely and one of the first things I did was stop the chimes in the sitting room clock. They were like a knell in the quiet heaviness of the parochial house where the faint trace of tobacco smoke and the heavy presence of theology books were sufficient reminders of life's realities without having every quarter hour of the rest of your life chiming away as you approached eternity in quarter hours grudgingly doled out to you by the Almighty. Francois Mauriac and Georges Bernanos had got it right. There is a special desolation about a presbytery inhabited only by a single priest who keeps his distance from the parishioners and a single housekeeper who must keep her distance from the priest.

So it was great when after about a week in the job I looked through the window one day and saw a car approaching and unloading four fellow priests, including the dean of St Malachy's College. They thought the townie might be lonely and came along to see to me. It was one of a thousand kindnesses I got from fellow priests and greatly appreciated.

My second job, a year and a half long this time, was as chaplain to the Mater Infirmorum Hospital in Belfast. Recently ordained young men were sent to hospitals as chaplains in those times, although we had no special training for it. It was straightforward enough if you were sent for in the middle of the night during an emergency, you knew what to do. But when you visited a woman of thirty facing death from cancer leaving a young family behind, you had to realise your inadequacy. Anyone would feel inadequate in those circumstances, and maybe being young had little to do with it. You gradually realise though that you do not have to go on talking to people, searching for words that are not clichés, trying to find meaning for what seems meaningless, the death of a precious being and the desolation of the innocent. Shared silence is sometimes a gift too. In the hospital mature patients knew only too well what life was doing to them. We often worried about whether we should tell them when nothing more could be done by medicine and death was coming, but we learned that people knew it, often knew it before we did. While we were worrying about whether we should tell them, they knew. I thought every politician and every cleric – and everybody – should be asked to spend at least one week every year working in a hospital. It would help us to get a sense of reality and priorities as nothing else would.

There were religious sisters in training in the hospital, preparing for the 'foreign missions', working long hours and getting no more than subsistence. Nobody got paid much in the hospital in those days, doctors, nurses or anybody. Theirs was an austere preparation for a future life which would take them to places where most people did not want to go.

I was surprised that one of the things a chaplain was supposed to do was supervise the once a week dance the nurses organised in the Extern and Casualty department. It was great fun for them but why on earth the chaplain had to supervise it was beyond me. I had long ago given up the idea of dancing as a way of enjoying myself – although some priests kept an admirable attachment to it for years to come – and I would rather stay in my bed-sit reading a book. I went to the dance a couple of times and then said I thought it would be better not to. Previous chaplains had attended and enjoyed it and this had become a custom. But the priest was looked on as a kind of supervisor too, even a kind of policeman in those times and it seemed people expected clergy not only to keep standards but to help enforce them. We must have made such a nuisance of ourselves when we could have been helping people enjoy life in their own way.

But those were times when people expected clerical intervention in their lives and some clerics were willing to supply it, even though it was more bother than it was worth and really trivialised a priest's life and work. High clerics expected to be phoned up by Catholics who had been invited to Friday evening dinners. Association dinners were often held on a Friday night, because members did not have to get up early or at all on the Saturday. But the law of Friday abstinence was in force in the Catholic church: no meat, but fish if you want to. So what were the Catholic attenders at a Friday dinner to do about not eating meat? Catholic law, with two thousand years of experience behind it, provided rationally for such things and the solution was proposed even by Paul of Tarsus who said guests should eat what was placed in front of them. There was no need to fuss. But people did fuss and some clerics in high places not only allowed them to fuss but encouraged them to do it. Hence the bizarre situation where men and women of some standing in the community would phone the bishop's house, or the vicar general's house or somebody's house and ask if at the dinner they should gently push aside the meat and ask for fish or could one without hurt to one's conscience eat the meat, with ecclesiastical permission of course?

The interpretation of church law in Ireland was often unnecessarily stern. To do what you are bound to do is hard enough, but to do more than you are bound to do and risk making yourself an oddity to your colleagues is even harder. And unnecessary.

Needless to say, unnecessary strictness invaded hospital ethics as well. People were not told how liberal and rational church law really is, and had to be, with all its 2000 years' experience. We all worried ceaselessly about birth control, abortion, fasting, even about pain killers when simple logic and good sense would have saved us time, effort and worry. Academic experts had become too isolated and were making life difficult for us 'ordinary people'.

While hospital chaplain I was also spiritual director of a Legion of Mary group down the road. They took care of girls and women who worked the streets downtown and around the port. They took good care of the women, went out to meet them in the streets, brought them in for an occasional rest, giving them advice, arranging breaks for them. Always in the hope that the women might change their way of life and find work at something else. At their meetings every week for prayer and reading and the assigning of work I had my first encounter with the Legion, got a great respect for it and never lost it. It was one of many groups of dedicated Catholics too little appreciated.

I was naive of course, and should have wondered that a young man fresh from ordination should be not only looking after patients in hospital but helping such experienced people as these to take care of women working the streets. And I should not have asked the question, one of the first I asked of the Legion members, 'What attitude do the peelers have to the women?' What I really wanted to know was why the women went on the streets and what the public authorities did about it. If poverty drove women to this work then poverty had to be tackled, not just the women. And if women did the work because they wanted to, there was little any of us could do about it. If men drove them to it for their own profit rather than the women's, then it was the men who had to be tackled. So what was the attitude of welfare workers and police? Why don't they all intervene?

The Legion members smiled when I asked about the police. The peelers are men and what do you think they do on lonely nights?

In those early nineteen fifties there was not much doing for peelers in the Belfast streets at night. Twenty or so years later it would be different and they would have to prowl around the streets encased in steel. I had not thought of the peelers as customers in the trade. There were of course always peelers going into pubs at closing time – seeing that closing time was observed and maybe getting a drink.

So the peelers were not going to do anything real. Nor the welfare people, except when one of the women got into trouble. And the oldest profession was not going to leave Belfast. But somebody had to lessen the hurt of those in it while the state just fined them or locked them up or ignored them. Now and again when we were growing up we would read in the newspapers that someone had been fined for 'keeping an unruly house', a delicate phrase which puzzled and annoyed us as children because we thought it too bad that peelers could have you up for not keeping the house tidy. So there was occasional fining for the street work, and occasional fining for soliciting or 'living on immoral earnings'. In this way the public conscience was satisfied and things went on as usual, the moralists condemning out front and shrugging complacent shoulders behind backs.

So apart from condemning, fining and confining the women to areas where they would not give the rich suburbs a bad look, there was little concern for those forced into it or alternatives for those who wanted to earn their bread in other ways.

The Legion people came close to two big issues then, poverty which drove people to selling sex in the chilling streets and their exploitation by men and women who made profits out of them. The indolence of the peelers made sense because they could not eliminate the business; they could only confine it and anyway there was a public demand which would always be there. They knew where the women were and as long as they did not encroach on areas in which they would be resisted and repelled either lawfully or unlawfully, that was enough, apart from any vested interest they might have in the women being around in the lonely hours of the night for their own comfort.

The Legion members were patient and during the one and a half years I was with them I never saw them showing impatience or disdain towards any of their guests. They used to go away for a day now and then to collect their thoughts and forget the city for a while. I went with them one day on an outing to Omeath. It was a beautiful summer day; crowds of people were strolling around the streets and down to the water's edge. We were heading down a little street to the water and suddenly a car came down, too fast, into the crowd, hit a couple and left the woman lying injured on the ground. One of the Legionaries shouted, 'She's one of ours'.

It was one of their guests out with a man, by chance on the same day and to the same place as the Legionaries' outing. They rushed to help her while the man she was with just disappeared. An ambulance came and took her away; her face which was heavy with make-up now smudged and miserable.

Next day I went up to Daisy Hill Hospital to visit her on behalf of the Legionaries who were at work; most Legion work was voluntary and part time. There she was, sitting up in a hospital bed, fortunately not badly hurt, as bright as could be, the cosmetics gone and showing herself as one of the loveliest girls you could imagine. If you felt anger it would not be against her but against the man who exploited her and left her lying in the dust. When she got well she came back to Belfast, visited the Legionaries who had helped her, thanked them and soon went back to work on the streets.

Another young woman they had welcomed into the hostel was less fortunate. She got cancer, went into hospital and had to have a leg removed. She might have gone into a corner and done nothing but weep for a life she could not live any longer, but she was too strong for that. When she got well enough she went back on the work again, wounded though she was. The Legionaries knew what was bound to happen now but the girl did not. When she went back to hospital after another year or two nothing at all could be done to save her life this time. The Legionaries sat by her bedside for as long as she wanted them. They arranged a rota in case she would need them during the night. In the early hours of a morning there was a phone call and I went to the hospital. The Legionaries had been there all night. The young woman they had cared for died that night, as near to being a saint as any of us are likely to meet.

Years later I met her baby, now a quiet solid man who had been around the world a good deal. He learned about his mother's death, saintly as it was, but nobody told him how she had earned her living to keep him when he was a baby.

After one and a half years in the hospital I was moved to the staff of St Malachy's College, only a step away round the corner but a world away in every other sense. The hospital overshadowed by so much sadness, good people worried and often distraught, paralysed sometimes physically and even more often mentally by the worry of what could happen to themselves and their families, the College with its bustling vitality, the hopefulness of young people, the intellectual vigour of staff and students. I was relieved to get away from the hospital, wishing that some day we would prepare men and women better to cope with the spiritual wonders of such a place. Now going into the College as Spiritual Director maybe I might be able to try it because I was going to look after university students who were on their way to be priests.

3

Teaching Religion

In 1951 I learned from the clerical grapevine that I was going to St Malachy's College as Spiritual Director. Some weeks afterwards I was told by the President when I asked him, and eventually got word officially to go there with a couple of weeks notice. Church business was like politics: changes were talked about casually among the few and after that people were told officially what was going to be done with them. When we reform the church, as we must do from top to bottom, or rather from side to side since there should be no top and bottom, doctrinal and policy decisions should be made by involving all who are concerned. We had an elite group of clergy we knew as The Club to which most of us did not belong and to which most of us did not want to belong. Some influential clergy did though. And that made them still more influential.

I looked forward to going on the staff of the College. One thing I was anxious to avoid – and even prayed every day it would not happen – was to be sent to a parish where money offerings were given at funerals. That was an historical hangover and an embarrassment in which the social standing of the deceased was often measured by the amount offered. Long after most of the clergy and a lot of other people wanted it removed it was still there in some country parishes, partly because of an understandable fear of how people might react at the first funeral where the thing was abolished. It is fair to plead that no money should be exchanged at any religious worship of any kind. People will always provide money for the church if they think the church is worth it, but collections at worship should be outlawed. Fortunately the funeral offerings were abandoned before I was sent to a parish as curate in 1966. And to be going into the College, not primarily to teach but to help students on their way to becoming priests was welcome. I went to tell the good news to my parish priest.

Father John O'Neill, the parish priest of my home parish, the Holy Rosary, was a decent man. They used to call him 'Bricks and Mortar' because he was one of the men who would be sent into parishes where there was building to be done. He gracefully combined the hardnosed abilities of a building priest with the courtesies of a gentleman. Having been sent to our Holy Rosary to get some renovations done, he was shocked to find the parochial coffers were empty. They need not have been; the parish was reasonably well off. But the previous parish priest, Dean Laverty, was not much interested in bricks and mortar and renovations were overdue. John started the renovations and having found the coffers empty, found also that some of the church decor was empty too. The contractors reported that the beautiful sandstone arches of the church were not sandstone at all but painted plaster. He unbelievingly climbed the ladder himself to make sure and realised that indeed this was one of those ecclesiastical abominations, one material dressed up to look like another. In some churches wood was painted to look like marble, cement painted like sandstone. It took another few decades to convince architects and clergy that everything in churches should be seen for exactly what it is. In the sixties a new generation of architects arrived who believed concrete should look like concrete and wood should look like wood. They wanted church buildings to reflect the truth and maybe even the unpretentiousness which should be the one of the marks of the true church. John did not like pretence.

He also had a modest and healthy respect for money and when I went to tell him about my new appointment he got his word in first. 'I hope', he said, 'they're not sending you to a College. They don't pay you.' I felt embarrassed at not getting my news in first but when he heard they were doing just that, he shrugged and said no doubt one should make the best of whatever you found in life, like it or not.

It was true they did not pay much, but in those idealistic years we did not mind. Priest-teachers willingly saw most of their salaries going into College funds to subsidise education for those who could not pay. We had enough to do us. Some years later when there was more state subsidy for education and College teaching staffs were earning better salaries, they asked to be given them rather than see them go into college coffers. Some began to be annoyed at the sight of Mercedes Benzs gliding up College avenues on Open Days and wondered why the clergy should be subsidising them. People were under a mistaken impression that subsidies were going the other way.

One of the great things about being on the staff of the College was that you could meet a superb intellect around every corner, staff or students who could match the best anywhere. I could call in to Donal at one end of the building and ask him to sing a song of Schumann or Hugo Wolf; at the other end I could hear an operatic aria or 'Roisin Dubh'. A lot of educational talent was wasted of course because students were made to study, and teachers to teach, what was chosen for them by panels rather than encouraged to search out what interested themselves.

Traditionally there had been a harsh regime in our College, a regime which men remembered even when they were in their eighties, their resentment at the harsh methods tinged with regret that those who suffered under them did not do something more to change them. I was lucky in that some of my Maynooth colleagues, Johnny and Frank and Joe and others, became members of the College staff also and tried to make the regime more gentle. But it was slow work for them. Traditionally 'grammar school' education was based on the idea that Roman and Greek cultures were the best of any world and had to be imitated in ours, that students had to be shown what to do, how to do it, and penalised if they failed to do it right. Educational ideas were harsh and there is plenty of evidence that the harshness was almost everywhere. The idea of free-flowing inquiry was far from the minds of most educationalists and from all bureaucrats. Discipline in education was often strict and sometimes vicious. There must be few men and women who passed through that 'classical' education in Britain or Ireland who did not have memories of its ineptitudes and the pains of enduring them. Put together the harshness of the classics, the theological anger of the Old Testament and teachers' fear of being judged inefficient and you have a mix which could destroy the best of them and it sometimes did. Fortunately most survived with dignity.

Going along the main corridor on the way to a religion class which perhaps one third of the students did not want to be in, most of them from a city which prided itself on being the most church-going in Europe and yet where church-going was a minority occupation, I met Fergus coming in the opposite direction, gown flying, head in the air, feet marching as if he was determined to defy the world, the flesh and the devil wherever they might appear. He was deeply religious. I asked him a question to which I had my own answer. 'Fergus, What are the marks of the true church?' He stopped, faced me, gathered the folds of his gown around him, sniffed and with no more hesitation than if he had been thinking about this very thing since breakfast announced: 'The marks of the true church are unity, holiness, catholicity, apostolicity – and an infinite capacity for self-deception'. And so he sailed on his way to teach students English and the art of debate.

The education courses they had to follow did not do justice to the superb intelligence of so many of the teachers and of students whose intellect was capable of developing and surpassing a whole world of education managers.

St Malachy's College had increased from a few students in dusty rooms in 1833 to about a thousand by my time, Catholic to the core. It developed in size, success and accommodation, and by the year 2000 had a greater proportion of Protestants on its staff than any of the non-Catholic Belfast schools had Catholics on theirs. But in the fifties and sixties we were just coming out from under the shadow of Catholics who sang 'A Toast to the Pope, the Royal Pope' and thought General Franco had been a soldier of Christ. Many of us now were reconsidering everything. As a new member of staff standing in a classroom which I remembered as Junior Five, I remembered also the disappointment I had felt as a first year at not winning the prize for a poem in praise of General Franco. And I shuddered.

My work now was mostly with young men studying for the priesthood in the diocese of Down and Connor. These men who would serve an area covering Belfast and most of the counties Down and Antrim spent the first three or four years of their studies taking a degree at Queen's. When I went as Spiritual Director in 1951 there were thirty five of them. The year I left, 1966, there were twenty five but as time went on after that their numbers dwindled until it was a blessed year when four new ones, or any, might arrive. I was also to help the spiritual education – and edification – of the other students, occasionally to stimulate or annoy myself and them by discussing religion and morals in classrooms, one of the most difficult places on earth to do it.

Years later I wished I could gather all those students together in the

Ulster Hall and say to them, 'Look, let's forget what we all said in the classroom and start all over again'.

Religion was the poor relation of every other subject in schools. Other subjects had examinations which students had to work hard for. There was an exam in religious knowledge but most students thought you did not have to work for it at all. Religion books were dull and turgid, and as the books for other courses gradually became more attractive, religion books tended to stay as they were. Religion should have been the most exciting subject on the school programme but by decisions outside the influence of the schools was constricted to aged concepts clothed in obscure words, not bearing the seeds of beautiful growth but echoing the war cries of battles long ago.

Years later religious knowledge was put into the state examination system and the standard of book production greatly improved. Under the old system young people were given some appalling questions to answer. One year they were asked to 'Write a Note on the Holy Ghost'. Questions were set by people we did not meet and answers marked by people who seemed not to take students seriously. The exam was inefficient, the results of one year being given to students the following year when they had changed class, age and perhaps even schools. Once into the state system there was greater efficiency but also exam papers and courses which in the tremendous effort to produce something acceptable to Catholics and Protestants (Jews and Muslims did not seem to matter so much) were so complicated as to daunt all but the most courageous of students and teachers.

The divine prohibition against despair was probably what prevented religion teachers everywhere from giving up as they offered religious knowledge to pupils, many of whom were less than willing to accept it. A member of staff trudging upstairs with a load of completed exam papers was asked by a colleague what was likely to be in them. He replied grimly, '90 per cent ignorance and 10 per cent heresy'. But he was already known for his pessimism.

Students and teachers knew it was in the home, in the community and among companions that we learn our religion and morality and that is where we make our decisions about them, not out of a school book set for school examinations.

With religious studies part of the state system, the possibility increased that students would shed religious education when they left school along with other things they thought they no longer needed. This happened in other countries too. So the church would need more and more a continuing, vitalising religious education programme for adults. We could not afford to put all our educational treasures into minds which were too small and fragile to satisfy the needs of their whole lifetime.

Still, our young people who were so casual about their religious classes and exams included many who in the future would go to the ends of the earth if necessary to do what they believed was morally right, and would do courageous things at home as well. Some of them were doing them already. There were teachers who taught religion well, worried over how well they were doing it, who knew that with a cynical world pressing in on them the young ones would have a hard battle to keep their balance, and that religion should be a strength to them, not a burden sapping their energy.

4

The Rights and Wrongs of Sex

One of the lessons we had to learn and teach was that faith, hope and respect for God and people would only flourish, or survive, if we took risks in generosity rather than fortified ourselves with law. That was a difficult lesson in Belfast.

Christians were created by a man who caused trouble by inviting so many excluded people to join him, yet they built an organisation in which it was considered a virtue to exclude people. Those women who worked the Belfast streets were excluded from what officious Christians called their society, and so were people of different religious groups like the Jews, even many fellow Christians. So all the more respect to those who courteously greet the women in the city centre and share meals with them, one of the most powerful signs of friendship, and all those who do not rely on exclusion of the weak for the survival of the strong. Our students were going into a world where generosity was often met by derision or spite.

And some of our preachers did a lot of damage to them. Belfast has a tradition of corrosive preachers, but hellfire and damnation preaching may have done less permanent damage than their preaching about sexual morality did. Into the two thousand year long stream of Catholic belief there had come what should have been unimportant little rivulets of weirdness but which poisoned the whole waters. The manichees, puritans, jansenists, fundamentalists all flung their stale bread on the God-given waters from which people hoped to get refreshing spiritual drink. We accepted too much of it.

Much of this preaching was based on the belief that pleasure was wrong and sexual pleasure most wrong of all. Adultery was said to be wrong not so much because of the injustice done to the partner who wasn't doing it as because of the unlawful pleasure of the one who was. Sexual enjoyment by oneself was condemned to young men and women who were waiting for somebody to tell them what they could do to help the millions of their people who had to live without food, let alone pleasure.

The intellectual and spiritual life of students could be clouded, paralysed, by constant demands by preachers to struggle against ideas – sometimes against ideas which they should have been worried not to have.

The body, they were told, is a constant spiritual danger to you; so is the world, the flesh and the devil. And while the faithful were vacuum-cleaning their minds, the hungry millions could wait. Young men whose intellectual and spiritual lives should be starting to flourish and blossom wrestled with phantoms, their decision whether to receive Jesus Christ in the Eucharist being dictated by whether they gave in to this sexual thought or said that sexual word. It was always stultifying, sometimes absurd.

Some of us decided that if this was Catholic teaching the teaching should be changed, and if it was not Catholic teaching the preachers had to be curbed or ignored. We re-opened our moral theology and church law books.

We gradually realised though that real Catholic moral teaching was not the enemy. There was a startling difference between what officious preachers teach, what real Catholic morality means and what Catholics believe. For every law in the law books and for most of the obligations in the morality books there was a string of exceptions. The fundmentalist preachers did not tell us that, for fear, they said, people might get lax. For instance, you had to go to worship on Sunday, but if you were ashamed of your clothes, or pregnant, or not well or if you could do it only at the cost of notable inconvenience you were not bound any more.

That phrase 'notable inconvenience' was fascinating. What excused you from keeping a church law was not unbearable inconvenience, not insuperable difficulty but notable inconvenience, inconvenience that would put upon you in a noticeable way. Instead of finding an oppressive moral code to attack, we found one which was more humane than even we had imagined, the result of two thousand years of trying to match the ideal with the real and finding a reasonable common ground between them. So what we needed then was not a new moral theology but a restatement of the best of the old one.

It was difficult though to convince people that we Catholics had a humane moral theology. It was difficult to discuss it with students without alienating parents and authorities who clung to 'good old theology'. The manichees, puritans, fundamentalists had done their work well and sometimes the very people who would have benefited most from a refreshed Catholic moral code were most insistent in refusing it. You could tell students and parishioners about it in private and many priests did. But that was not enough. Preaching had to change if it was to be faithful to our faith.

A small group of priests met informally in Dublin to find ways out of their dilemma. They could take refuge in the Catholic principle that while such and such a thing was a serious breach of the moral law, it was less blameworthy, maybe not blameworthy at all, because of a person's circumstances or state of mind. This could help people get rid of some of their fear, but it was not enough. A feeling of futility and uselessness was heightened, not lessened, when a person was told, 'What you are doing is wrong but you are too weak to do anything else and so you get a sinner's pardon', which looked like a fool's pardon as well.

To bring matters to a head in our own small world we approached a canon lawyer and asked him a question we thought worthy of the Scribes and Pharisees: 'Tell us, when a husband and wife have sexual intercourse tonight will they be better persons for it, or worse persons or spiritually just the same tomorrow?' We were trying to get him to admit that their sexual intercourse as an expression of love was good and therefore a virtuous act. Some of our people would not approach the Eucharist after it without a penance. We said we would not press him for an answer today but would ask him again tomorrow. Next day he said he did not wish to discuss the question.

We thought Jesus Christ would have done better than that with the Scribes and Pharisees. He might have left them to work it out for themselves but at least His answer would have been more clever.

In the year 2004 the Vatican gave credit where credit was due and said much of what we asked our friend the lawyer to say fifty years before. But by that time it was a bit late.

Some Saturday evenings Ben used to come visiting. He worked in a retail store downtown. He taught me about of the horrors of the life he and his friends had to lead. They were among the excluded. They had to live in frustration and secrecy. There were crude jokes about them at every turn, on radio, in films and theatre, on the streets, in conversation, in schools. Preachers used the story of Sodom and Gomorrah to shame them, the vengeance of God to threaten them. Some of them were deeply religious, some delicately artistic, all of them normal. The fear-filled hatred of them by fundamentalist religious put them in perpetual danger of attack while the quiet contempt of so many other Christians forced them to be constantly furtive. We had created fugitives among our own people and Ben was one of them.

All this was in the mid-fifties long before the gay communities began to recover their self-confidence. He was fortunate because some good people, including priests like the Redemptorist Sean O'Riordáin, helped Catholics to understand their plight. These made all the difference between an abiding sadness, sometimes self-destructiveness, and a living that was at least tolerable. On one hand Sodom and Gomorrah thundered with the threat of hellfire, on the other was the medical treatment given to homosexual people because they were said to be victims not of a cruel society which refused to recognise their dignity but of a disease which could be cured if the victims went the right way about it.

The right way proposed was often horrifying. Quietly and without the hatred he could have felt, Ben told about the aversion therapy given to him and others who accepted that they were ill rather than normal. Taken into a 'mental' hospital, shown pictures of naked men, given drugs to make them feel sick as they looked at them, in the hope that this connection sown into their minds between naked men and sickness would cure them of their desire to see the one for fear of suffering the other.

It did not work; it did not deserve to work. One futile effort after another was made to deal with people who were different and were in mental agony because their own people, nearly all of them Christians, had decreed that difference was dangerous, sexual difference an abomination. Cruelty mistaken for kindness.

In the fifties and sixties the gay communities had not dared come out openly and rebel against these things. Men and women had been driven to despair, some to suicide, some to religious scruples that made a peaceful spiritual life impossible.

Ben had a perceptive mind and good friends who brought him through the worst of times. He left his shop job and became a teacher himself. In the College on Saturday evenings we talked about music and art and gossiped and drank a glass of wine and he helped me to understand.

I suggested we should go out somewhere for a meal one Saturday evening. He knew a good restaurant in Carrickfergus. In the restaurant a three piece band was playing. After a few numbers it stopped and a spotlight shone on the tables one by one. The leader of the band made remarks which were meant to be funny but were only tedious and offensive. The light swung round and shone on our table.

'Oh', he said, 'Look at these two. And what may I ask are these two fellows doing dining out together all alone, eh, what's happening here, eh?' I felt a fierce anger. I half rose and Ben grasped my arm. 'Don't do anything', he whispered. 'I know what I want to do with that clown.' 'Don't. Just do nothing.' The spotlight swung away, the music started again, and we were eating ashes. 'Let's go'. As we left Ben said quietly to me, 'Now you know what we have to put up with all the time.'

Ben and his friends had still to find a way of life fitted to their needs and potential rather than to the moral constructs of garret-bound academics – with laws that will put them at their ease and their persecutors out of business. I wondered how many students in our colleges would benefit when that happened.

5

The Challenge of Christian Unity

Church students were told in the mid-fifties that within fifteen years the Catholic church would be facing a crisis. They would be the priests most affected by it. The timing was close; in 1970 for the first time Catholic youths incensed by the British government and their church leaders told a Catholic bishop in the streets of Belfast to 'fuck off home'. There was always some anti-clericalism in Ireland and more was bound to come. It had happened to the church abroad and must happen in Ireland too unless there was some factor in Ireland to prevent it. Some argued it would not happen in Ireland, that Catholic priests in Ireland came from the wide Catholic community rather than from some elite class and therefore would escape. But on the other hand, no matter where they came from priests were taken aside and educated in seminaries where the distinction between clerics and lay people was emphasised just as strictly as differences between management and workers in big industries. None of us foresaw the church scandals of the future which would not create the problem of anti-clericalism but would hasten and deepen it.

By the nineteen nineties it had become socially acceptable, almost socially required, to criticise the Catholic church in Ireland. Those who had seen it coming in the fifties and sixties were proved right. When church officials at last became conscious of what was happening, they decided to ride out the storm rather than cure the reasons for it. They believed in letting as many as wanted to go depart and then from the solid base of faithful Christians remaining a new evangelising and conversion would begin. That was the theory.

Perhaps it was the only theory likely among people who believed that not only time but eternity was on their side.

By the fifties and sixties then the churches were keeping their political influence but losing their followers; a new world was coming in which they would have to decide afresh what they wanted to be and to do. They were all divided into traditionalist and innovative camps, the first having free rein to say what they pleased, the second cautious, wary, often silent when they wished they could speak and always few in number. Among the church leaders many of the old fears and angers remained and blocked new radical thinking.

Persuading officials of the different churches to stop abusing each other seemed a practical although minimal starting point for those who wanted change. Getting them to leave aside their internal arguments and cooperate to do away with poverty and unhappiness would be a suitable continuation. Both were tried and often met with surprising indifference or opposition.

I was in a privileged position. I had space to write in, students and staff in a college to talk with as well as clerical friends, opportunities to broadcast.

It was by chance in 1959 that I had got involved in a series of conversations with Protestant clergy which went on for many years. This was through Father Hugh Murphy who was one of Ulster Television's religious advisers and also a chaplain to the Port in Belfast. He had once persuaded me to celebrate Mass in an empty shed in the shipyard; I do not know what he hoped we might achieve. He was the only Irish priest I knew who had a photograph of Queen Elizabeth in his sitting-room. Bishop Dan Mageean had asked him to be chaplain at the Port and part of his duty was to take care of Catholic members of the British Navy who might be around from time to time. Hugh agreed but went a little further and joined the Royal Navy Reserve. When Dan Mageean met him later at a clergy retreat in St Malachy's College he remarked that while he wanted Hugh to help the people in the British navy he did not expect him actually to join them. But as far as Dan was concerned it was Hugh's decision and was all right. Hugh used to attend Armistice Day commemorations and other events like that but none of this softened the attitude of unionists who years later kidnapped him, threatened him with death and kept him imprisoned for a couple of days. They seemed to think that by capturing a priest they would force the IRA to give up a policeman they had captured.

One of the duties, or perks, of Hugh's job was a naval training course on the Isle of Wight. While he was there he got a heart attack. Word came back home that he was worried about not being able to attend a meeting he had arranged with Reverend Jackson, a retired Presbyterian minister. He asked me to go to the meeting in his place, offer his apologies and talk with him. This was the first of a long series of meetings with Catholic and Protestant clergy and I cannot remember any of us refusing to meet any of them at any time during the next forty years unless it was impossible.

Those meetings probably helped change personal relationships, but official church attitudes remained as they were and clergy most of the time acted publicly according to official attitudes rather than personal conviction. Most of the time we just had the modest ambition of getting church officials and church members to treat each other and each other's beliefs with respect. We made friends and maybe helped break down the propaganda that our friendships should be limited to those who agree with us. We were very aware that friendship could not be constructed; we were under no more obligation to like Protestants, Jews, Muslims or humanists than to like Catholics if we did not appreciate their company and it was the same for them. Trying to make a friend of a Catholic or Protestant, Jew or Muslim because of his or her religion was just as irrational as making an enemy of them for the same reason.

Protestant clergy were powerless to make changes because of the influence of the secret societies to which so many Presbyterian and Church of Ireland clergy belonged. The influence of the freemasons over them was as mysterious as it was meant to be. However liberal or friendly these clergy might be, they knew and we learned that important decisions about relationships in churches and politics would be made by these societies, not by our conversations.

So in the nineteen fifties, sixties and seventies we met as many people as would talk to us and discussed Christian unity and the ways to create a peaceful and equal society. We brought people together as much as we could. It took time and energy and was often frustrated by the official churches' apathy, public fear and anti-Catholic organisations. And by some church people who agreed with the work but wished either to control it or let it die.

Hugh Murphy and I saw the opposition's power and other church people's weakness close to us when we had to abandon meetings with church groups, his with Methodist friends, mine with Presbyterians. Paisley threatened to bring his followers on to the streets to demonstrate outside their clergymen's houses. We withdrew from two publicised meetings when we realised it would have embarrassed and damaged the Protestant clergy if they were seen to withdraw their invitations, but it would not damage us in the least to thank them and courteously decline to accept. Professor Jimmy Scott of Queen's University was right, though, when he said we should all have stood together at that time, in the mid-sixties, to tell Paisley to shove off, using the language he would have understood, when like any bully he would have had to do so. Later was too late. We discovered during the following years how wise Jimmy's advice was but without unity among the gentle Christians, the bullies flourished.

I met the Rev. Jackson as Hugh Murphy had asked me. We talked and arranged further meetings. Hugh slowly recovered in the Isle of Wight and came home safe and sound but not equal to the hectic pace of life he had had beforehand. My involvement with what we called the ecumenical movement increased and all efforts in it were enhanced or hindered by the quality of church leadership.

People were integrating naturally by working together, through marriage and education and going to live in each others' districts. Integration through work and living beside each other however was often frustrated by the Orange Order and similar associations, while integration through marriage and education was hindered by Christian church policies. We soon learned that we could bring people together all right; the trouble was keeping them together in face of such grim determination to split them apart again.

6

Appointment of Bishop Philbin

In 1963 William Philbin was appointed our bishop in Down and Connor. Clergy were surprised, even dismayed. We were puzzled that he was taken from his small diocese in the West of Ireland where some joked that he could communicate with all his clergy by shouting out of the window. Cahal Daly would have been a more popular choice. The Roman bureaucracy are inclined towards those who have a strong connection with Rome, perhaps as students or post-graduates. The Papal Nuncio as the Pope's representative in Ireland has a lot of personal influence. Priests are asked in occasional polls to nominate three men they think are bishop material but their opinion about the appointment of William Philbin seems not to have been taken into account. Most of them would probably have preferred Cahal Daly and would also have preferred a priest of their own diocese as second choice. A bishop coming 'from outside' is always in a delicate situation.

The political reasons for William Philbin's appointment seemed clear enough. He was sound on the EEC, the European Common Market, which would evolve into the European Union. Sean Lemass, Taoiseach at the time, was moving Ireland in that direction. In Britain there was opposition to joining, even to the extent of British governments helping to set up a rival organisation, the EFTA (European Free Trade Area), but William Philbin had written in favour of Ireland joining and this was a political mark in his favour. Also, the government in Dublin accepted, unwisely, that 'the troubles' in the northeast were due primarily to Catholics and Protestants not being able to live together in peace. William Philbin, they believed, could have an influence for peace, coming 'from outside' rather than from Antrim or Down or Belfast, he could take a more detached view of what was happening and could help to lessen antagonisms.

The clergy had a more realistic view than the Dublin government of what caused bad relationships in the northeast, and a more mature view than the London government of what needed to be done to heal them, but in appointing bishops, bureaucracy speaks to bureaucracy and the wisdom of the people is silenced. The northern problem would not be greatly affected by a bishop being agreeable with Protestants. It would be influenced by bishops and others being strong enough to force good government for everybody on an unwilling regime. Whether Cahal Daly would have been strong enough to do this was not put to the test this time.

The clergy received the new bishop with their customary courtesy, whatever reservations they had about the appointment. They knew it was not going to be easy for him. He was courteous but detached. He was different from Dan Mageean who was bishop for about 25 years before him. Dan was a strict administrator who insisted on things being done according to the book. His visits to parishes were rigorous and clerics joked that he was known in Rome as the one bishop in the whole world who actually carried out the Roman regulations about marriage documents. But once his official duties on parish visits were done, Dan would join in a meal and conversation, a game of cards if there was one, a cigarette often hanging out of his mouth as he gave and took a lot of geniality. His was a hard act to follow and William Philbin could not be expected to follow in Dan's footsteps.

In Maynooth as professor of Dogmatic Theology Billy Philbin – Phibs as he was dubbed – had two reputations among students: one that he was a brilliant lecturer with a brilliant mind, the other that he was dull often to the edge of boredom. It was agreed that he was distant and did not easily make relaxed friendly relationships. The Maynooth system required students and teaching staff to keep their distance from each other. If students wanted to talk to a professor outside class hours they had to get permission from the Dean of Discipline. This protected most of the professors from most of the students most of the time. In Maynooth if you did too much of anything – seeking out professors, studying, lazing, or even praying – you could be suspected of being 'singular', a serious matter which could lead to your being asked to go elsewhere. William Philbin therefore had spent much of his priestly life shielded from people, even from those with whom he was professionally involved.

With this background he was bound to find life difficult in a busy, crowded and uneasy diocese. He started out by assuring priests that he would be open to them and with them, willing to meet and talk with them when they wanted it, something which, given his personality and previous experience, must have been difficult. He was polite and learned and made a good impression on priests who in turn welcomed him.

He got an early blow but not from his clergy. It was during one of the earliest spiritual retreats for priests he attended in the College. He left the retreat for a few hours to go and visit unionists and other public representatives at the City Hall. Some clergy were uneasy. They believed great caution was needed when dealing with unionists, many of whom could be nice to him in the morning and undermine him in the evening of the same day. If he had taken advice from enough of the clergy he would probably have postponed that visit and certainly would not have left a clergy retreat to make it. But on this as on other matters later the advice he accepted was inadequate.

Before long he came to understand how caution, care and good advice were needed before entering the northern political arena even for courtesy visits. He also learned how the church policy of trying to achieve change through interaction between church hierarchy and the government did not work. He later had bitter exchanges with the unionist administration about schools and the Catholic-managed Mater Infirmorum Hospital, about anti-Catholic discrimination in the Sirocco works. So he was caught between his desire to create understanding between Catholics and the ruling unionists, the clergy's fear that it was at worst impossible and at best extremely difficult, and his personal experience of the rudeness which prominent unionists thought was proper to offer Catholics, however elevated their position. Like all the clergy in the northeast he had to choose between the perhaps impossible task of creating friendship with the ruling unionists and a possible task of defending and encouraging Catholics to demand fair government from them – and the even more difficult task of combining both. It was our version of the biblical dilemma of serving God and Mammon at the one time.

The quality of advice senior clergy gave him was crucial to his choices. When a Protestant cleric asked how they could create better relations between the churches, one of the bishop's senior advisors said, 'Well, you could get your people to stop burning our people's houses for a start'. This was not Philbin's way; he would have been more diplomatic, even to the point of not insisting that the houses were burning at all. In time he seemed to depend for advice on the more forceful of senior clergy who had their own anti-socialist, anti-republican politics and were deeply suspicious both of unionists and of Catholic laypeople. He was in unfamiliar territory and needed guidance through the political and religious minefields from people who had been there all their lives. Some nationalist politicians were approved and allowed to help him but most were frozen out. In a situation where Catholics needed as much cooperation and united effort as possible that church policy failed. Dan Mageean had been strongly independent and yet open and clergy-friendly. William Philbin found it difficult to be as strong as that.

Some of us perhaps expected too much of the spirit of renewal and freedom which seemed to lie behind the Vatican Council.

In 1963 we invited Gregory Baum to come and talk to a public meeting in the College Hall, everyone invited, especially those clumsily referred to at that time as 'our separated brethren'. For Belfast it was an unusual meeting in unusual times. Baum had been brought up in the Jewish faith and had become a Catholic. Now he was an internationally known scholar and adviser at the Second Vatican Council. What he said and wrote echoed what Simone Weil wrote with its deep longing for a better life shared by everyone. Simone Weil was Jewish and lived on the edges of Catholicism for years but she did not join the church. Baum did and worked to promote renewal within the church and reconciliation among Christians and between Christians, Jews and others. He came to us on the way to Rome from his home in Canada.

The College Hall was packed with many of our friends from different religious traditions who gave him a friendly reception. He did not say anything world-shaking, but then he was not expected to. We were just glad of someone of his intellectual stature to encourage the movement which was developing in Belfast as people moved towards each other as friends, not opponents. That movement was giving us hope in the nineteen sixties.

When he finished his talk, before the questions began, I noticed a friend of ours, a Presbyterian minister, leaving the hall. I went out after him, afraid he might not find his way through the quad and along the corridor to the front door. I also wanted to ask him if he would like a cup of tea. No, he was in a hurry. I did not think of offering him anything else; to a Presbyterian minister where was the use in offering anything more exciting than a cup of tea?

The College Bursar appeared behind us and taking our friend by the arm, asked him, 'You'll take a wee something before you go?' What a significant difference there is between a cup of tea and a wee something before you go. To my surprise our friend said, 'Yes, that would be nice'. So I left him with the Bursar and more than an hour later, when questions and most goodbyes were over, I found him still with the Bursar, still in the dining room and still enjoying a wee something before he went. For all our ecumenical meetings the Bursar knew more than I did about clergy, and what he knew was not from ecumenical books. In the nineteen sixties the most vital discovery we were making was not what our friends believed but that they were normal.

As I was coming across the quad when all was over another clergyman joined me. I said, 'That was good, wasn't it?' He said, 'Yes, it was good'. And then he added, 'I never met a Jewboy yet that didn't have the gift of the gab.'

The shock of that statement made us realise what a long way we had to go and the public lectures, ecumenical meetings and academic discussions might just be skimming the surface of a racist society in which even the best of people may be either indifferent or guilty. Beneath the surface of respectability there was still a deep vein of disrespect which would take a long time to dissolve. Being normal still meant being able to say something racist and not noticing you said it.

Next day we brought Gregory to Maynooth College. They received him with their usual courtesy. Opinion was sharply divided about him there though, and no one doubted that the Irish Catholic church beneath an apparently unchanging surface was beginning to shift just as uncomfortably as Christians elsewhere.

In the sixties it was thought daring to have people like Gregory Baum giving public lectures. He was severely critical of what Cahal Daly and some other fellow Catholics were writing about birth limitation and such things. Creating open discussion not only between Catholics and others but even within the Catholic church itself was an uphill struggle at the time. And yet there was such a history in Ireland of people dissenting from state and church policies that we were simply trying to keep a tradition alive, not creating a new one.

When Bishop Philbin returned from a session of the Vatican Council he asked me about Gregory Baum's visit. Nobody had asked his permission for the lecture – we were trying to get away from all that – and he probably felt affronted. I told him, 'He was good, but he did not say anything revolutionary'. He replied, 'That's good. I'm glad he didn't '. And we left it at that. We did not discuss the possibility that what was normal elsewhere might well seem revolutionary in Belfast. Shortly afterwards the bishop made his only visit to our church students and warned them about the hidden dangers of ecumenism.

Even with all the drawbacks and limitations the nineteen sixties were a time of change and we thought we should be part of the change. The Second Vatican Council was on, there were student revolts in Europe, the civil rights movement was gathering pace in Ireland, people seemed to want change, even people who had seemed unchangeable themselves.

There was a lot of fresh thinking going on among Christians in Europe and the Americas, ideas which could carry the church wherever the Spirit led. The Vatican Council from 1962 to 1965 was not to call halt to this but to select what it saw as acceptable and reject the rest. Even with that restricted aim significant change was possible and Pope John XXIII seemed to want to renew the spirit of the church, brushing away old accretions and refreshing everybody. But there are powerful bureaucrats in the church, and conservationists, not just conservatives, conservationists too, who think the old ways are always best even when they do not work. Optimists thought everybody's hopes and fears could be met, pessimists that change would ruin the church. Struggling for influence and power in the church went on for years during and after the Council, absorbing energy which could have been better used.

Early in the nineteen sixties Cahal Daly published a book about natural law morality. As Spiritual Director of the College at the time I was interested; other priests were worried too about the effect current moral teaching was having, especially on students. Terry O'Keefe, editor of the Irish News, sent me a copy of Cahal's book and asked me to write a review of it. I would have expected an academic to review it but I agreed to do it.

When I sent the review to him, he accepted it graciously as usual and asked if I wanted to have it published under my own name or as 'a special correspondent'.

I thought the by-line was an editorial decision, not one for me, and was content for it to appear either way. He was concerned about official church attitudes to people expressing independent views. A Catholic professional man in Belfast wrote articles about the church for the Irish News but gave it up when Bishop Philbin objected to a mild reference he made to people not being happy with the slow pace of change resulting from the Vatican Council which went on fitfully between 1962 and 1965. The writer knew from experience when he was beaten, even by shepherds who appear like sheep. In the unionist regime many Catholic professional men depended on fellow Catholics, including church officials, for work. They had to be careful about whom they might offend. So the rest of us had our choice, either keep quiet and hope for better times, or confront the censors.

Terry published my review of Cahal's book under the by-line of a 'Special Correspondent'. The result was unpleasant. Clerics were not supposed to criticise what church officials did, or what church experts said. Cahal, like Gregory Baum but with very different opinions, was an expert adviser at the Vatican Council and my review was critical of what he wrote. A junior priest doing that must appear unsound. But the Second Vatican Council was going on and a wind, or at least a breeze, of change was supposed to be going through the church. In Belfast we wanted to create free discussion, assent and dissent, each respected. I soon heard about dissatisfaction and even anger about the review. Younger clergy seemed not to mind but some senior clergy were indignant about it, and nobody knew who had written it.

I should have been flattered by the rumours of the writer's identity, academics as far out of my range in the intellectual ratings as could be imagined. The review was not profound. It was simple, not a great intellectual adventure, to say there had always been differences of opinion in the church, there had always been corruptions in society and great condemnations of them by ardent Christians, so our times were hardly any different from any other and there were plenty of writings to prove it. The trouble was that if we believed ours were exceptional times we would then be given to believe that only exceptional people could deal with them whereas we wanted the potential and talents of all the people to be brought out to deal with them. The times were ordinary, the corruptions were ordinary, the theatre was ordinary, the morals of the cities were ordinary by the standards of what had been experienced before. That being so, ordinary people had to deal with them. After all, we believed the Holy Spirit was in us all. And the message of Jesus had been given to 'the multitudes', so if you wanted to learn what the message was, it was to 'the multitudes' you should go. The review did not say all that but that was the notion behind it.

Eventually the secret about who wrote the review came out and I was blamed for not having signed the article in the Irish News. I explained that whether my name appeared over the article or not was an editor's decision, although to tell the truth I would have been uneasy if I had opened the Irish News one day to find the article with my name there on top of it. Church officials believed you should say what you were supposed to say, and only when told to say it, and any other way of doing things was frowned on. But that could too easily make us like a political party where a chief whip puts a beady eye on people and brings them into line like little dogs at a hunt. Anyway, whatever damage was done was done, and I could not believe anyone would be the worse for it, especially Cahal who had both the intellect and the friendship to deal with it.

That incident underlined our dilemma in a time of change. If you were asked to write or broadcast or make any comment in public you had a choice: say what you believe is right, whatever the consequences, or fit your statements to suit your future. A clerical friend once told me when we were talking about the need for change in the church that he was going to do or say nothing to upset his career. That was the only time I had heard priesthood described as a career. But there was no sense asking students to form and express their own opinions if you yourself were only going to say what was pleasing to those in authority. You would soon have no need of being censored; you would censor yourself. There were plenty of people in Belfast whose living, and sometimes lives, depended on not saying things. Those of us who had even a limited independence then had all the more duty to use it.

That review may have increased a feeling among higher clergy that I should be put where I could do little harm. I got no information about this since like most clerics I did not belong to 'the club'. What was certain however was that whatever Cahal felt about the matter, he was still a friend and remained so. Wondering about anything else was a waste of time.

The affair died down. Shortly after publication of the review I heard from a fellow member of the College staff that I was likely to be 'shifted'. He knew more about clerical chat than I did so I supposed it might well be true. I was indeed shifted but that was not until a few years later, in 1966, to St John's Parish in West Belfast.

Meanwhile rumours about what was happening in the church abroad flowed around us, fuelled both by those who encouraged change and those who dreaded it. Newspapers and broadcasters had their own agenda so one of the best ways to find out what was really happening in other countries was to go and see.

The College summer holidays gave us an opportunity to go abroad for a few weeks in the year. Some College priests went to work in parishes abroad, some stayed at home. I wanted to find out two things in particular: whether what we were reading in newspapers and hearing at our ecumenical meetings in Belfast was true, that there was near revolt in Dutch Catholic churches, and that Protestants were persecuted almost to extinction in Spain.

I went to Madrid and one of the first things I noticed in a street was a building occupied by a Protestant Evangelical Society. If what I was told by Protestant friends in Belfast was true, no such thing would be there, or if it existed it could not be in public view. The important thing was not that the building and society were there but that respectable people in Belfast were telling me it could not be. The fact was that if you wanted Protestant literature in Madrid you went into a shop and bought it.

We were often told at our inter-church meetings and in church notices in Belfast newspapers that Protestants were persecuted in Colombia. I could not go there but thought that if people misrepresented the situation in Spain we could take what they said about Colombia with a grain of salt as well. The truth was that

Catholics, Protestants, humanists and many others were persecuted and impoverished in Colombia but the persecution of humanists and Catholics seemed not to matter; the important thing was for one Christian group in Belfast to score points off another. The fact that tens of thousands of Catholics and others had been persecuted and killed in Spain because of politics, religion and property did not seem to count either. For many Belfast orators the important struggle – the only struggle maybe – was between Catholics and Protestants, not, for example, between fascists and democrats, between greedy and needy.

We were expected to become outraged by what was happening in the Church in Holland too. The church there, Catholic publicists said, was on the brink of revolution, or schism; the ideas circulating there could tear the whole church into factions. People talked about schisms who had not used the word since their religious history classes. It seemed sensible to go to Holland and find out. I asked my mother if she would be willing to come along. She was fond of travelling and said 'yes', so off we went.

To Amsterdam of course. And to Knokke a seaside town in Belgium on the way. Someone there told us Knokke got its name because an Irish saint brought his Christianity to it about 600 A.D. The name Knokke came from the Irish word 'cnoc', meaning 'a hill'. We could not see a hill anywhere. Maybe an imaginative or homesick Irish missionary called the place after some hill at home. Or maybe in a moment of impatience he had done away with one that was there.

On the road to Amsterdam we went into the first Catholic church we came across. In the porch there were posters advertising pilgrimages to Lourdes, just like we would find in the churches at home, some of whose senior clergy were saying the Dutch church was on the verge of schism. Inside this church we could see something stirring, so maybe we were coming on some evidence of this revolution in the Dutch church, some strange new rite perhaps made up of this, that and the other, designed to please as many people as possible, a Dutch goodbye to the institutional past and hail to the future?

As we waited for it a priest in a black soutane came out, knelt in front of a statue of Our Lady, a small congregation knelt behind him. He started five Mysteries of the Rosary. We had come to Holland in search of a revolution; we found the Rosary instead.

There was, however, a lot of thinking going on in the church in Holland. People there had come through the second world war suffering horrors; many of them were put in prison, Christians found companions of all kinds in those jails: communists, humanists, Jews, separated Christians. After the war many of them decided that the old divisions – in Holland they were perhaps even stonger than in Ireland – were wrong and they must now build an integrated society. By the nineteen sixties those who disagreed with this had marshalled their forces and the arguments went on: should they go back to the old divisions, a Catholic radio, a Protestant radio, Catholic press and schools, Protestant press and schools, or make a break with the past and unite for everybody's good?

They were asking more fundamental questions too. Does the church really have the power to declare marriages valid or invalid? Does it have the power to forbid priests to marry, or the power to declare some things impediments to marriage? The debates were lively among the academics and writers while among the Catholic population at large life went on much as before, with a checkerboard pattern of conservative parishes next to changing ones, people changing or not while the academics' questions became more and more irrelevant to what people really did with their lives.

One day we went to Mass in a Dutch parish church. As we sat for a while after the Mass a man came out of the sacristy, a fine brown suit on him, matching shirt and tie, a fawn raincoat over his arm. I whispered to my mother, 'That's the priest who just said Mass'. She was startled and at first did not believe it. Clerical dress was only slowly slipping out of use in Ireland where a priest could still be sacked for not always wearing it. She had listened with patient tolerance to what she had heard about changes and questionings in the Dutch church, but found difficulty at last in a priest dressed like a man about town.

To find out what was happening to the church in France you did not have to go there to find out. French people wrote about it themselves. But we went anyway. The church had gone so far downhill that already by the nineteen forties there were parishes where not one person was normally attending church, even in the countryside, even in the Pyrenees near the sacred shrine of Lourdes and this had happened without the church hierarchy knowing it. And trust in the church was going downhill too. A school teacher in a Paris suburb when asked whether he sent his children to the local Catholic church school, said warmly, 'Certainly not. They're all Marxists there'.

Decline of the churches would happen in Ireland too; it seemed inevitable we would go the same way as the continental European churches had gone. So it was easy to foretell even as early as the mid-fifties that the Catholic church in Ireland would be in crisis within about fifteen years. Church hierarchies did not take that seriously. None of us foresaw the worst crisis that would develop in Ireland. It would not have been surprising if it had been about inefficiency, waste, loss of belief, millionaire lifestyles of some bishops, about finances of the church managed as if it were a business, but the child abuse was surprising, frightening and unforeseen.

When Pope John XXIII died in 1965 the Union Jack over Belfast City Hall was flown at half-mast. That came as a shock to many of the citizens. People said it must be a sign of how good Pope John was that he should get such a tribute from the city fathers of Belfast. On the other hand, some unionists in Belfast in the mid-sixties were looking for a reason to be nice to Catholics, some even wanted changes, a few wanted radical changes, and the death of Pope John gave them an opportunity to make a civilised gesture. The flag at half-mast may have been less a tribute to Pope John whom Protestants knew little about, and more a gesture to Catholic neighbours about whom they were getting to know more. Either way we were glad of it. It was a nice thing to do.

7

Blessed are the Poor

I was sent as a junior curate St. John's parish, West Belfast, in 1966 and stayed in that position until 1975. It is an almost entirely Catholic area and has mostly nationalist and republican politics.

I was assigned Whiterock and Westrock, two housing estates adjoining Ballymurphy. Westrock was a collection of prefabricated asbestos and metal dwellings put up, like those by the banks of the Lagan on the south side of the city, at the end of the second world war. They were said to be temporary dwellings but they lasted for decades. 'Lasted' is hardly the right word. They continued existing and gradually fell into disrepair, helped in this by a city council policy of neglect. The surroundings were dingy and unhappy but the interiors of the houses were well kept, apart from a few residents who found it impossible to cope. Official and unofficial propaganda said the residents there would not keep their homes and children clean, a constant slur by comfortable people against those they needed to look down on. In the housing estates in West Belfast there was a constant struggle to make ends meet, to live with dignity in spite of official neglect.

West Belfast and Ballymurphy in particular have always been under attack of some kind. Belfast Corporation jerry-built the Ballymurphy estate after the second world war and put tenants into it, many of whom they had already labelled unsatisfactory. After that they dubbed it a problem area and people could condemn Ballymurphy and district without restraint. The housing estates around the greater Ballymurphy area were treated the same way. The refusal of authorities to help the people of our district was always a nuisance and often insulting. We were living in a world of two respectabilities, respectability which could be achieved by money, and respectability which would not be recognised because people were poor. Some of the things people said were absurd, for instance that people from our area did not feel as badly about being in prison as others would, that if our people would use their money better they would be better off, as if carefully using next to nothing would make it into something. There was courage and self-sacrifice but the world outside seemed not to want to know.

In the fifties, sixties and seventies the money lenders were hovering on the edges of the district in big cars waiting outside post offices for repayments of their loans and to re-take possession of benefit books, in an area where employment was refused and then people were blamed for being unemployed.

Abusive propaganda against less well off people is constantly used by government and its supporters; An Officer's Wife in Ireland. a booklet first published in the nineteen twenties and still circulating among Protestants in Ireland during the nineteen nineties, was saying the same kind of things.

Sometimes local priests tried to counter the propaganda by pointing out the unfairness of the attacks. But we realised that while many comfortable people needed to have people to look up to – state or church royalty – they also needed someone to look down on. As one Belfast housing estate was built after another the last one built became the most abused. When I was a college student Whiterock was the scapegoat, but later it was Ballymurphy, while Whiterock was then described in comparison as relatively good. It had been good all the time but in cities there has to be a social scale which often follows the shape and quality of housing and the latest comer is often awarded the lowest place in public esteem.

We had to protest against journalists' reports which gloried in describing degradation. People in our area did more to help themselves than people in any other Belfast area I knew about, and such journalistic cynicism hurt us all. One journalist had said, among other things, that Ballymurphy had the biggest incidence of VD of any area in the north of Ireland. He was lying, but statements of that kind sold papers for him and made some people feel good. A time would come when praising people in Ballymurphy would help sell the same papers and therefore praised they would be, but in its early days it was not like that.

Many of the residents had photographs on their mantelpieces of soldiers, relatives who had served in the British forces. British soldiers coming into the area ravaging people and houses from 1970 should have been puzzled by being ordered to raid houses where the occupants had so often been on their side when they needed them. The intellectual quality of the soldiery, like the integrity of their government, was too low for that. As a raw curate in 1966 I could see the quality of the people living there. They treated clergy and church with courtesy which seldom failed.

Fr. Cahal McQuillan was assigned Ballymurphy. Senior church officials did not seem to realise the work priests of his calibre were doing or how much help they needed or the plight of the people they worked for, or the immense fund of goodwill there was for the church in those times. I saw the goodwill often, dramatically sometimes. One evening in the seventies when the armed conflict was at its height, I was brought to attend a young man who had been shot in the back by a sniper shooting from Corry's wood-yard. As I left the house where he lay, a group of women surrounded me and went with me along the street. The women were protecting the priest with their own bodies. They would have done it for anyone, but especially for a priest even though he belonged to a church institution more and more unwilling to recognise their courage and goodwill.

Cahal was not listened to much by bishops although he spent himself trying to get improvements in his part of the parish. Once when Bishop Philbin came on an official visit, instead of asking Cahal to escort him around this most impoverished area of the parish, he asked the youngest and recently appointed priest to do it instead. We believed he did not want to face the problems there. Cahal came to my room afterwards almost weeping with frustration; there was so much to be done, so little help to do it. We talked about how he was not working for any bishop or hierarchy but for God and the people. Nobody had to tell him that; he knew it well. But the work, anxiety and strain were intense for him as they were for many others like him. One day when I was away in Castlewellan with Ernie Strathdee doing something for UTV, we got a phone call to say Cahal had become suddenly ill and died.

The most severe armed conflict was in the seventies but the people of Whiterock, Ballymurphy, Springhill and their neighbours had a lot to endure long before the years of armed abuse when military and police could arrest anyone in those areas because there was a public assumption of guilt or inferiority against them. The most hurtful thing they had to endure all the time was neglect by those whom they had considered their own people: people in the South of Ireland, people in the universal church. All our church wealth, international connections and influence did not prevent a single death, a single arrest among our neighbours, did not reduce the suffering, did not soften the ridicule. When bishops confirmed the neighbours' children they told us the Holy Spirit was granting wisdom, knowledge and the rest of the sacred strengths to these people who needed all of them. How hurtful it was then that when they used this wisdom, expressed this understanding, showed this fortitude, the response even of those who had confirmed them was at best silence, at worst condemnation.

When I came to St John's I thought I would be asked to say Mass and do other things in the Irish language, and wished I had had more notice so as to work up the Irish I had. I need not have worried. I was not asked to do anything in Irish for some years to come.

The Irish language had been a poor relation in our primary and second level education. Some of the most brilliant teachers were teaching it but textbooks were dull, even by the standards of educational dullness at the time. When more attractive textbooks began to appear for other subjects the Irish language ones still lagged behind. Public authorities and many schools did not treat the language with the respect it deserved as they overshadowed it with English, Latin and Greek. Belfast students went to Donegal to learn and enjoy it. I never went even when a College colleague, Dr. Joe Maguire, ran ceilidhthe and other functions to raise money to bring them there. The students brought home stories about Micky Sheáin Néill and Huidí Phaidi Huidí, and talked about the conquests they made or thought they made with the girls.

In West Belfast in the sixties little of the language was to be seen or heard in public. Nobody asked me to say Mass, conduct a marriage or baptism or funeral in Irish. It was as if the language could be spoken in private, in Cumann Cluain Ard, the Ard Scoil or other quiet places, but was not being publicly celebrated. The cultural revolution came later. West Belfast had a strong cultural tradition and you were reminded of it when you saw Elizabeth Begley on stage or on the road, or nodded hello to Joe Tumelty as he strode up or down the road, always ready to tell you about this stream or that street like the best of guides.

But there had been such hard times. The parish had layer upon layer of people and their families who had been driven out of their homes in the twenties, thirties, forties, and fled here. They could point out where the huts and tents had been put up to shelter the refugees of each generation. The twenties, thirties and forties had come and gone; now in the mid-sixties people were drawing breath, preserving their traditions carefully but not flaunting them. It was going to take a lot of work and many years and tears before Irish language and culture became a matter of well publicised rejoicing. In the mid-sixties we could not see a future in which bilingual theatre would be commonplace, when the bookshops would display books in Irish as fine as any, when there would be Gaelic-speaking schools, when parents, teachers and pupils could read their Irish language newspapers and the Falls Road would have so many places where they could do their business in their own ancient language. Before all that happened the foundation of the Gaelic-speaking village in Shaw's Road in the early seventies seemed a cultural miracle.

Not being asked to do anything in Irish I felt at once relieved and regretful. But we had successfully washed away so much of ourselves.

You could go into churches in the city and find inscriptions in Latin, Greek and a wisp or two of Hebrew, but no Irish. A furious controversy had arisen in Dublin in the fifties about compulsory Irish and what a nuisance it was, but no voice was raised to question the years of compulsory Latin or Greek which had been forced on generations of students. As Padraig Pearse complained, people were starved of their own mythology, language and history and had to make do with other peoples'.

But times change and in the nineteen sixties there was little Greek, while Latin was losing its popularity with educators. By the year 2000 young priests when asked to celebrate Mass for the Latin Mass Society would refuse because they said they knew no Latin. By that time it would be hard to find a Latin textbook in Belfast bookshops but in the city centre and on the Falls Road there was a multitude of attractive Irish texts. While compulsory Latin was disappearing from church and school, discouraged Irish was alive in the restaurants.

But cultural poverty was only one side of a general poverty in Belfast which was obscene. In College we thought we knew a lot about life, but going into parish work I realised how little I knew of the poverty in which so many of our Belfast people had to live. Many of them belonged to one of the richest institutions in the world, the Catholic church. The church had international connections, money, universities and two thousand years experience dealing with political and economic regimes of every kind. But for the people in West Belfast and a multitude of others the church might as well have been an impoverished, unconnected heap founded last Thursday, they got use of so little of its resources. So we had to ask: how can we get use of church resources to which the people are entitled, to let them create the prosperous dignified life they are entitled to?

At that time we could have built a factory for £65,000 and could have used the church's international contacts to fill it. There were plenty of workers in West Belfast only too willing to fill any factory that might open. If you preached a sermon asking for money to build a shrine or a cathedral you would get a good response from people with money to spare, but building a factory was not so attractive, or maybe people thought certain things, like work, were beyond the ability of those who lived in what they described as 'underprivileged areas'; perhaps they thought there is a managerial class, a professional class, a class of people able to do this, that or the other and our neighbours did not belong to it. Sometimes people shared this view. I asked a mother in the parish why we should not provide the business people, doctors and nurses and clergy and lawyers we needed from the people of our own district. She replied, 'Those things are not for us'. But ideas change and eventually she herself took on three poorly paid jobs all at once to help give her children the education they wanted to become 'professionals', highly qualified people who could hold their own anywhere. It takes a while for people to recognise that everything is for them and nothing is beyond them. But before that time came for us a lot of blood was shed and a lot of hurt suffered. It should not have come to that.

A Quaker friend was indignant when anyone talked about 'underprivileged areas'; what people were doing without, she said, was not privileges, it was their rights.

At that time there were few places in the district where people could meet and talk about whatever they wanted to talk about. You could rent a schoolroom or hall if the school managers agreed but in the sixties when a bishop referring to the civil rights movement could say, 'Don't be led by the Reds', they were suspicious about who was talking and what they were talking about. You could hire a hotel room for meetings but there were few hotels and little money to hire them. So we urgently needed a space where people could come and talk freely, where nobody had to ask anybody's permission for meeting, where you did not have to refer a simple request for space to a committee and wait days or weeks for their answer.

That was the main reason for renting and opening the house which became the Springhill Community House in 1972. People needed space in which to be free. Renting a house in the newly-built Springhill estate was a small part of the answer. It lay within the parish boundaries in an area of appalling unemployment. I went downtown one Saturday evening and pushed the first week's rent for number 123 Springhill Avenue through the door of the Corporation Housing Department in Adelaide Street and it felt like small liberation. The biggest room in the house could hold about 15 people comfortably, and a few more uncomfortably. We had a kitchen, a small room for a library and two rooms above these. We needed talk and we needed self-confidence and we needed work. It seemed the people would have to find all of these for themselves.

In number 121, the house next door, the Ballymurphy Enterprises cooperative started up, created by the combined efforts of local people, professional advisers and helpers. During the following years while we were held our meetings and education classes in 123, Ballymurphy Enterprises set up its machines next door and made knitwear. A Russian journalist arrived at the House one day carrying a brief case in which among other things he had a bottle of Vodka and asked, 'I'm not sure if the Vodka is a suitable gift for a Catholic priest'. I assured him it was not unknown and he went in to see the machines next door. As he went round he murmured, 'It is just like the great Russian revolution'.

The Ballymurphy Enterprises cooperative soon left those small premises and headed out up the road to new premises specially built with the aid of whatever grants and loans they could get from a reluctant government.

Ballymurphy Enterprises however went bravely into a highly competitive market. A friendly manufacturer in the south, when asked his advice, said the profit margin for his own knitwear business was often as low as two and half per cent. You needed two things, superb efficiency in the factory and superb marketing outside it. The Ballymurphy Cooperative was at a disadvantage working with old machines, the only ones they could afford. Old machines break down too often. The manager, skilled as he was, could only go so far with them and however good the workers, the superb efficiency they needed was just not possible. The manager had to see to the flow of goods in and out and had to fix the machines as well or find someone else to do it. And he had to go out looking for orders, so while the shop floor was being looked after, the marketing would suffer and while the marketing was going well. the shop floor might be working with one or two crippled machines. The superb waste-free, high production efficiency and marketing to make a profit with a two and a half percent margin were difficult if not impossible. They needed new machines and extra staff, and for that they needed capital and capital was hard to come by.

We would never say any cooperative failed. Cooperatives never failed. Even if they went out of business people learned so much, especially about their own abilities and about the kind of competition they were going to face. That experience was important in West Belfast and became more important in time.

People who set up cooperatives soon learned also that those who worked in them did not necessarily want to manage them. The way workers were treated often made them want to take control of businesses. But many people, probably most people, did not want to be managers. They wanted to work but not necessarily in management. If they saw an opening for themselves whereby they could own and manage they might take it but most of the time people wanted to do a day's work which would still leave them time to do the things they wanted to do in their own families and community. Management might help them do this but it might not. They had the right to choose.

The important thing was the opportunity for dignified work.

I was never any good at managing anything, so I could understand why most people did not rush into management, even in cooperatives, but I could make suggestions, some of them impractical.

A lot of money was flowing out of the district, money we needed to make our district what we believed it could and should be, one of the most beautiful and most prosperous in Belfast. So I suggested we should have not only a knitware cooperative but cooperative licensed premises and bookmakers and bingo sessions as well, with profits returning to the community, but all that fell on deaf ears.

The Black Taxis, founded in the early seventies, succeeded in keeping millions of pounds inside West Belfast which without them would have flowed out.

The Whiterock Industrial Estate also started in the early nineteen seventies, an imaginative project taking part of an old farm in the district to develop as a cooperative people's industrial estate. The committee creating it was set up by professionals and local people. The professionals, architect, lawyer and others, had rebuilt Bombay Street, burned out by police and unionist civilians in 1969. The Whiterock Industrial Estate could create perhaps 200 jobs but the British government made sure this would not happen by sending in the troops to occupy it in 1979, putting the management and workers out at gunpoint. It had been in existence for about five years. The military did not leave the place until the end of the nineties and it has never yet recovered its lost energy.

Having rented an empty council house in Springhill in 1972 what could we do with it? Live in it! Father Hugh Mullan, a fellow curate in St John's, had good ideas about how we could help our neighbours. He wanted to bring in furniture to be sold cheaply in the school hall during holidays. I hoped he could work that scheme because I would not have a notion even where to start. We had both agreed we should get out of the parochial houses on the front of the Falls Road and live in a house in the newly-built Springhill housing estate. That fell through when the bishop said it was a bid by the two of us to 'take over that end of the parish'. It was not of course and we had followed proper church procedures to get the house, passing our proposal through the parish priest to the bishop. The Corporation allocated the house to us at a public meeting and this was reported in the newspapers. Senior church officials reacted by deciding that our plan to live in it was off. The response came back from the bishop to the parish priest, then to a senior curate and so to us. There was no consultation with us about it.

Hugh Mullan decided not to go on with our plan. I said I would rent the house as a base for people to meet in anyway and we would go on living where we were for the time being. I think it was five pounds I pushed through the door in Adelaide Street for the first week's rent.

Some time later the parish priest Father Hugh was living with asked him to find somewhere else to live. A house was bought for him in one of the few owner-occupied areas in the parish and Hugh went to live there. When internment night came in 1971 the people in that area were pinned down by gunfire. Hugh left his house to help neighbours who had been shot and was shot dead himself. That street, Springfield Park, was devastated then by unionist attacks, so yet another brave experiment by Catholics and Protestants living together in peace was shattered. Houses were abandoned and residents fled.

When a new curate was appointed in Hugh's place there was a difficulty about where he would live. He could not go to Hugh's house in Springfield Park and houses elsewhere were not plentiful. I took the opportunity and suggested that since I had been allocated a house in Springhill by the City Council I could move into that one and Hugh's successor could move into my rooms in the parochial House on the Falls Road. This was agreed. Maybe in the confusion of the times church officials did not think very deeply about it.

Now I could live in the house, but what was to be done with it apart from that?

The following years were difficult for everybody. There were attacks, gun battles, military and police abusing people; anything people tried to do was liable to be disrupted, postponed, abandoned. And we had an almost empty house. I say 'we' because there were always plenty of people around able and willing to help. It was lonely at first, as it is for anybody going into a new house not knowing the neighbours. There were few telephones in the area at that time and people needed phones, often needed them desperately, so when we put in a phone, neighbours came in to use it. We could offer little apart from empty space because we did not have the means to provide anything much else. Gradually people came in and talked.

Noelle Ryan, who had worked with church organisations in Liverpool and with Frank Duff in Dublin, came to Belfast in the early seventies and under her management the House came alive.

For some years we had had a small Social Action Group in the parish and we learned from it that if a few well meaning people get together and decide what is good for other people, what they decide will probably not work. People do not need to be patronised; they know their own business well enough. What the House offered then was a little free space and gradually more people accepted it. Some came in to use the telephone, others came to get a bit of peace from what was going on outside, others came to offer help to neighbours who needed it and, very important, people came in to talk to each other. One day a neighbour from 'the Bullring' in Ballymurphy said she would like to do something about her reading and writing. I thought she had a literacy problem. She had a problem all right, but the problem was that she was already writing stories and poems for her children and wanted to do it better. She and others began studying English language again. Gradually the House became an adult education project with groups studying Irish, English, other languages, maths, politics, religion, history, sociology and whatever happened to be around. The neighbour who had been writing for her children wrote sketches for the theatre when it came about, acted, advised and helped others, sometimes to read and write, most times to do it better.

As our people tried to improve their lives, founding cooperatives, looking for employment, they were treated with indifference, often with disdain. Ballymurphy Enterprises had to close because of lack of capital to invest in it. Whiterock Industrial Estate was closed by the military who took possession of it at gunpoint. They had plenty of space to build their barracks nearby but chose instead to enter and occupy the only sizable industrial area in the district. When we opened yet another at Conway Mill down the Falls Road they threatened to destroy that too. So not only did they refuse to create development, they destroyed developments the people tried to create for themselves.

That was the hurt. The insult was the way people were treated while all this was going on. In the mid-seventies Michelin advertised jobs and we offered them our Springhill Community House to hold their interviews. A long queue of men lined up inside and outside the house far into the street looking for those jobs. It was like something from the time of the hiring fairs. Over a hundred men looking for jobs and as it turned out only one job was available. When I wrote to the papers about this long queue in search of work and the one job there for them the only unionist comment was, 'You must have a fine big house to fit all those people...'

We searched for a space to open a small workshop which people could have free for six months to work out their own ideas for work. Once that six months was up they would either be successful and go to other premises or would see their idea was not good enough and would leave the space for someone else. That was the plan, the kind of plan we could carry out without much money. Going up and down the Falls Road it was surprising to find so many people working in old garages and outhouses, making doors, mending cars, selling carpets. To our amazement there was no suitable empty space available for a workshop. We asked LEDU (Local Enterprise Development Unit), a government-funded body for job creation, if they would build some small new basic units so that those who were already working could go into those better premises and leave the old worn-out spaces for others up and coming. They refused. Their answer was not only negative but insulting. They said they would do that in other areas but not in ours. No explanations necessary. That was policy. At that stage we realised we would have to get space of our own totally under our own control. That made Conway Mill so important for us some years later.

We did not realise then that LEDU was destroying not only our efforts but those of others more important who had more potential than us. In the early seventies a firm named Clokeys, glass makers, wanted to come back to Belfast. They had been in West Belfast for years, were burned out during riots, and now had a factory making extractor fans in England. Not many people at that time wanted to come back. They contacted LEDU. I was asked to go over with a LEDU representative to talk about the situation and about whether the local community would support Clokeys. The LEDU representative and I travelled first class on the ferry to Liverpool, the first time I travelled first class on a ferry. We met Clokeys and all seemed set for them to return home to set up business again in West Belfast. About three weeks later I got a phone call from them asking if I would tell LEDU please to get back in touch with them. They were irritated that

LEDU had not done so and the caller on the phone remarked that LEDU might at least acknowledge that they had given us lunch. Nothing came of it and we saw then the mixture of indolence, unwillingness and inefficiency which made government-sponsored development in Catholic areas impossible.

A businessman up the road said that in his experience, 'As far as LEDU is concerned we don't even exist'. He moved to Dublin where the commercial climate was better and would eventually lead to the Celtic Tiger.

Later we learned that with some people brown envelopes would determine the shape of things to come, or not to come. But there was nothing we could do about that because people who benefited from it would not come forward and say so while those who did not benefit were powerless.

In areas like ours the money wasted, the false assertions made, the unproductive decisions by government-sponsored bodies and others should have been recognised as a public scandal. But this was Belfast and they were not. Refusal to build units for those who wanted to create work, refusal to follow up offers of business, refusal to help cooperatives desperate for capital, sending in the troops to destroy what little industry there was, that was normality.

The combination of insult following injury might have stifled the spirit of the people but it did not. Along with the sustained propaganda attack on our neighbours even by politicians who scarcely knew the place and hardly ever visited it there was an economic attack as well. Due to our friendships with people abroad and in other parts of Ireland we got to know about conditions in a lot of places which often resembled our own, and were often much worse than our own. We learned from the World Health Organisation that workers in some tea plantations were so poor that they had to send their children away in exchange for money so as to get them a decent life and education.

So when we were instructed on social justice by, among others, an Irish millionaire tea merchant that seemed just as bizarre as it was likely to get.

8

Death of the Sixties' Hopes

In 1963 there were too many clouds on our horizon. Changes were coming in church and state and we could make our choice, be part of the changes, resist them or do nothing in the hope that the demands for change would go away. Priests made different choices. Those who joined civil rights marches went in ordinary dress because church authorities did not approve of them. Some founded the Association of Irish Priests working for better relationships in the church, for due process, that is, adequate procedures by which people could openly put their case if they were in dispute, and for an enrichment of all church life. When the Association gathered strength the Irish bishops responded by setting up a priests' association of their own. This was usual, to create a parallel association rather than openly oppose the first one. The first association faded, the second remained and engaged in officially approved activities from then on.

Priests as well as others were becoming more aware of their rights in both church and state. Up to the mid-sixties Catholics in the north of Ireland had to search for decent unionist representatives and ask favours of them; in the mid-sixties the mood changed. The civil rights movement stopped asking for favours and demanded rights. That was a revolution whose seriousness the reigning authorities recognised. Inside the church there was a movement, small, unobtrusive, which required justice and equality and paralleled the broader movement for civil rights. Some priests were involved in both movements, and church hierarchies disapproved of both. The hopes symbolised in the Second Vatican Council helped the clergy who were involved.

Most of us thought the Second Vatican Council (1962-5) would encourage better communication between people of different – and no – religious beliefs. That did happen but the main purpose of that Council was different from what many commentators said it was. For decades there had been new thinking in Europe about religion and church law and relationships inside and between churches. If this fresh thinking had continued without restraint it could have led to a cultural and intellectual revival of Christian life which had been soured by the tawdry struggles of the post-reformation period. But it was not allowed to continue without restraint. There were people struggling for power in the churches – those who believed the only rock solid basis for survival was refusal to change, those who believed change is necessary for all normal human life and lack of change means stagnation, not stability.

'If we want things to remain as they are, things will have to change.' The Second Vatican Council, whatever Pope John's ideas about it, became not just an encouragement of new ideas but a means to confine and control those newly emerging ideas which conservative churchmen thought unsafe but had to tolerate.

However, for all its limitations which would appear in the following years as groups within the churches struggled for power, the Council by its very existence encouraged people in Ireland to try to heal the divisions which had been exploited among them for political and financial gain. We thought if we could heal religious divisions in the northeast we could solve the problems not only of our deliberately damaged social relationships but of inefficient government and bad economics as well. People were indeed brought together in peace, especially in the changing political and religious climate of the nineteen sixties, but we did not realise how vain this would be unless and until we dissolved the power of the secret societies which government and churches had used to frustrate the natural friendliness of the people.

Before I left the College for St John's in 1966 I was hoping there could be a radical review of education by the church. I thought church leaders should withdraw from the formal education of most children, leave it to other voluntary bodies and the state, get suitable compensation for whatever buildings and facilities they left and use it

to create a fresh programme of education for adults and for others
with very special needs. If we did not do that many young people
would abandon religious education and practice on leaving school. It
happened in other countries; it would happen in Ireland. Anyway,
worship of God is a matter for adults and young people should be
introduced into it as developing adults not induced to leave it as if it
were just part of their childhood. We needed an adequate continuing
explorative education for adults. Times were changing and what
young people did and thought was going to be shaped by what they
experienced outside the schools rather than inside them.

Schools, colleges and seminaries tried to mould children into
perfect adults. But perfect adults grow; they are not produced in a kind
of moral assembly line. In other countries young adults got rid of
things they believed belonged only to schooldays, like going to
church on Sundays. Education by clergy or religious did not prevent
this happening; it may even have encouraged it. French priests in their
soutanes who shepherded children through streets or into zoological
gardens and youth centres were eventually discarded by young people
who thought they had outgrown both the school trips and the men who
led them. So, shifting most of the education resources of the church
from children to adults seemed logical. If adults continue their
cultural and religious education we need not worry about the children,
but well educated children do not necessarily grow into educationally
mature adults. The idea of lifelong learning became popular in the
sixties but seemed not to capture the imagination of church people.
The state controls curricula, methods and financing of children's
education and the churches have little real influence on its content or
its effect. So there is good reason for them to use their educational
resources for adults and for those who are still disadvantaged within
the state system, whether children or adults. Churches can afford to
experiment and have plenty of talent with which to do it. And part of
the experiment must be the free flow of ideas.

Christus Rex, a priests' association for social studies founded by
Cahal Daly and others in the fifties, seemed a useful place to talk
about that. I was disappointed though. When talking to the
Association about continuing adult education I said we should use all
available modern means of communication for religious education
and discussion in parishes and everywhere we had a chance. This was

at a time when even a parish film projector was rare. Someone in the audience asked: 'If we had these resources what would we do with them?' At the time I thought this was just a put-down, but maybe not. It was frightening to think that perhaps what we lacked was not the means but the message.

Modern means of communication were not going to be provided from our parish funds and very few priests I knew had the money to buy them for themselves. Most priests, contrary to popular belief, were in debt for years. One city parish priest said if a parish newspaper did not make money he was not going to allow it to cost the parish any. When I suggested at a clergy meeting that there should be a diocesan newspaper in which the bishop could give his message, this was dismissed, not by Bishop Philbin but by one of his influential advisers with the remark, 'We are not going to have all kinds of people saying all kinds of things.' People were going to say all kinds of things anyway, and when some years later the need for a diocesan newspaper was accepted, it was not a success. It also was too late and did not reflect the excitement of a people who had faced the world for two thousand years and survived.

There were so many good ideas in the church waiting to be released; there were talents, there was money; what seemed to be lacking was our courage to put forward fresh ideas, to experiment with them, to cultivate an ethos of free discussion in which friendships or clerical promotion would not be put in danger from it and to use money according to faith and not according to feasibility studies. And perhaps most of all the gift of being able to recognise that the time had come for courageous moves, for trying on ideas for size in a church that had either to change or to wither. And we of all people could afford to make mistakes.

Bishop Philbin often said to us, 'Change for its own sake is not good'. Not many of us were looking for change for its own sake but even if we were, change just for the sake of changing is necessary to keep up our morale, whether we are caring for a shop front or a family. We are always changing things and being the better for much of the change. We say the Holy Spirit gave us 'discernment of spirits', the ability to know right from wrong and the faith is passed on not just by books or lectures or schools or sermons, but by living words between living people, by the way we live and explain the reason for it when people ask us face to face. Maybe we were secretly afraid of what our message really meant or whether it could really be explained; better call it a mystery and leave it unexplained.

The idea that church people should voluntarily give up schools to the state, ask compensation for buildings and use the money to start up a new education in the faith for adults and especially those in difficulties was exciting but not generally accepted. Neither was the idea that if there must be huge blocks of flats in our city we should hire or buy one floor in each of them and let that be the block residents' chapel. As time passed from the clerically confident sixties towards the doubting end of the century these ideas seemed less bizarre as great church buildings lapsed into cold gloom with the loss of congregations, the quiet departure of priests or their failure even to appear.

As Springhill Community House came alive around the mid-nineteen seventies, it gave us a chance to experiment. The education project was for adults, not for children and we hoped it would be controlled by the people who used it. We did not foresee, or hope, that parents would come asking for education for children too. But they did.

Voluntary projects for children not at school, expelled or staying away in Belfast were of two kinds: those which went seeking the children and those which, like ours, were for adults and whom the children or their parents sought out themselves. In the nineteen sixties and seventies it was easy to expel a child from school in West Belfast and we all suspected that in the quest for good exam results some schools were content to get rid of children they thought would not get those results. In some schools excellent results were to be seen at one end of the spectrum while there was an invisible shedding of pupils at the other.

What we were looking for was learning which broke through the barriers which controlled its free movement. In Springhill we tried to invent new forms of discussion, open forums, public inquiries, discussion sessions, theatre, days of quiet retreat, while other new associations were being created in Belfast whose aim was the exchange of ideas without anybody's permission. The Platform Group was one, the revived Newman Association at Queen's which was drowned when the political upheaval came in the early seventies. The Open College and the Ulster People's College were attempts to break through the inhibitions from which people had suffered for so long.

The Open College was started in the centre of Belfast at a time when fewer and fewer people were venturing into the city centre and it closed after a few years. Dave and Beth Rowlands who founded it often had faced bleak times for that imaginative project. One evening when the People's Theatre was giving a performance in the Open College in College Square, nobody came. It was the only time we had ever had nobody for an audience. That was in the mid-seventies and the quiet of the deserted street was even more disturbing than any amount of riotous noise. Then through the night air came the sound of footsteps. A man turned a corner and walked towards us. As he came near we had to be careful not to alarm him; it was that kind of time in Belfast. I asked him if he would like to see a performance by the People's Theatre. He asked how long would it take. I told him and he said, 'All right', and we had one man for an audience.

Belfast often had to offer free seats to audiences. Sir Thomas Beecham once became very angry in Belfast when a concert by the Halle Orchestra got such a small audience because of a boxing match the same evening. Sometimes promoters went out into the highways and byways to get people in. The free-seaters had to be sure how long the concert would last, especially in the days when pubs closed at ten o'clock. John Mc Cormack sometimes had his audience increased this way; the customers got a free show, all was safely over by closing time and John was heading up the Lisburn Road on his way home while those of the audience who were not worried about closing time were crying out for a last encore.

During the sixties there was a lot of contact between people of all kinds, north and south: politicians, clergy, business people and others. Many of them seemed willing to make the best of the existing political situation in the hope that civilised living would lead to a permanent and better solution with a dignified part for everybody to play. Those meetings made us hopeful. I went to a meeting in the Republican Felons' Club on the Falls Road. The members talked about changes in politics and church and what they could do to help them. As I left the meeting I asked who their next guest was going to be. It was a prominent unionist politician. It must have been a time of opportunity when men and women who had suffered appalling prison regimes were inviting unionist politicians to come and talk with them and they were willing to come.

One of the new associations was PACE, founded in 1969. The name PACE stood for 'Protestant and Catholic Encounter' but was also a play on the word 'pace' meaning 'peace'. We hoped PACE would help to raise the hopes and dissolve the hatreds of the time. It was inspired by James Scott and his wife Olive. They invited people to their home who believed a new vision was possible for politics, religion and much else.

James was Professor of Dental Anatomy in Queen's, a brilliant man, poet and political writer. He had become a Catholic at a time when other brilliant people were doing it too and becoming unpopular with some colleagues as a result. He wanted to see Ireland united by consent and had a deep respect for those who thought otherwise. At that time in Queen's and other unionist strongholds there were a few people willing to break through its stifling conservatism. Jimmy was one, Dickey Hunter was another but in a different way. Dickey became a Catholic too. He was a brilliant superbly qualified medical graduate but turned his back on academic advancement, earned a lot less than he deserved and went around Europe between terms organising circus acts. His circus appeared every year in Belfast's Grand Opera House. Dickey would enter the circus ring cracking his whip, top hat shining and boots gleaming. Most of the audience did not realise that when he was introduced as Dr Hunter he deserved the title better than nearly anybody else in town.

James Scott would sit at the founding meetings of PACE leaning forward on the walking stick which relieved some of the awful discomforts of his arthritis, would listen to long intense conversations about agonising decisions and would murmur patiently, 'Do you know, I must be unique here; I've never had to make an agonising decision in my life'. The people he and Olive gathered together had been putting forward ideas of respect and cooperation during the previous twenty years, an interesting and moderately hopeful crowd with a lot of very varied opinions.

Denis Barrett was a member of the Society of Friends, the Quakers. J.J. Campbell was a Catholic who worked with Denis for political and religious regeneration. Campbell had tried to join the Unionist Party. Another member of the PACE group, Brian McK McGuigan, had joined him in this attempt by a few Catholics to test the sincerity of Terence O Neill and the emerging liberal wing of the Unionist Party.

These emerging liberal unionists seemed to be coming round to the belief that Catholics should be worked with rather than exploited. Applying for membership of their Party was one way of testing them. The applications were refused. McGuigan was a solicitor, Campbell head of a department in a Catholic teacher training college, later to become a professor at Queen's.

Canon Barry was editor of the Church of Ireland Gazette a constant critic of the Catholic church, even the broadcasting of the Angelus bell being a matter of constant concern. Another founder member of PACE was Canon Eric Elliott of the Church of Ireland, one of whose themes was Protestant fears and Fethard-on-Sea. I heard about these so often at various inter-church meetings that I resolved never to visit Fethard-on-Sea, the ghost hovering over every discussion between us. We also had Jim and Miriam Daly, two university lecturers, both of whom later became members of the Irish Republican Socialist Party. The Presbyterian Professor Jimmy Haire, the Methodist Rev. Eric Gallagher, the Presbyterian Rev. Desmond Mock, G.B. Newe, Monica Patterson, Jack Sayers who in effect invented the liberal unionism which gave us some little hope, Stanley Worrall of Methodist College were also members. Eric Gallagher had been President of the Methodist church, Jimmy Haire Moderator of the Presbyterian church. G.B. Newe became the first Catholic member of a latter day Stormont cabinet, Desmond Mock became a proponent of anti-Communist politics, and Miriam Daly was assassinated by unionists in the hallway of her home.

Another founding member was Rev. Alfie Martin who had been Presbyterian Moderator in 1966. In that year he summoned a Stormont cabinet minister R.W.B. McConnell to the Presbyterian Assembly and gave him a politically fatal public wigging over his failure as Minister of Home Affairs to protect the Assembly from a Paisleyite mob. McConnell accepted the telling-off with bowed head and retired from politics, not to re-emerge until decades later when he was given a seat in the British House of Lords. I remarked to Alfie that this episode was like the Catholic bishops summoning a member of the Dublin government to Maynooth to receive a politically fatal telling-off from them. The big difference between the incidents was that the Catholic one would never happen without a public outcry of protest, including one from the Presbyterian church. He maintained the two cases were different but I could not see it.

All of us met often and talked a lot but made the mistake of believing that if we brought Catholics and Protestants talking together we would solve political problems. The fact was, and it took us a while to realise it fully, we could bring people together as often as we liked but when their coming together became politically inconvenient for the regime, the secret societies and especially the Orange Order would split us apart again, if necessary by assassination. Our people so far from being unable to live together in peace were so good at it that the government had to take such appalling measures to split us apart.

Bringing people together was only one part of the solution. The missing part was a programme of dissolving the power of societies like the Orange Order. And we did not acknowledge the importance of all our people, not just Catholics and Protestants. We could bring people together but only government could dissolve the power of the secret societies; and those secret societies were the government's most powerful supporters and agents. For all the clergy and others joining PACE or otherwise bringing people together there were more powerful people splitting them apart again.

We thought of PACE as reducing tension, part of our preparation for a future democratic society. It was not as some thought afterwards a counter-revolutionary plot organised on behalf of the government. It was bitterly opposed by fundamentalist Protestants and other government supporters.

PACE groups were formed in and outside Belfast and founder members often went to speak at their meetings.

This was not always pleasant. Coming up to Christmas 1970, the season of goodwill, Eric Gallagher and I were speaking at one of these meetings in Newtownards, County Down. People described as 'gospel revivalists' picketed the meeting outside and heckled us inside. They were about 40 per cent of the audience. The verbal attack was mostly against the Methodist Eric who was accused of not preaching the true Gospel. I was considered beyond redemption apart from a miracle of grace. The accusations and verbal abuse were accompanied by cries of 'Alleluia' and 'Praise the Lord'. One member of the audience however described the demonstrators as 'political dinosaurs who could not think for themselves'. A Newtownards newspaper headed its report of the meeting 'Gospellers Attack Ards Group'. Things like this did not happen often to PACE speakers but then they were not often going into areas where antagonisms were so high. When it did happen one had the feeling that it would have been better to stay at home because reason had given way to carefully fostered hysteria.

In a mission hall in Belfast the gospellers shouted, praised the Lord and heckled us; somebody called in British soldiers and policemen and they came in and lined the walls. It was difficult and tense but I was treated gently enough, most of the anger being heaped on those who were seen as betraying Protestantism by having the likes of me around at all. When things got rough and the hecklers were not getting the best of the exchanges from floor and platform someone in the hall shouted for the anthem 'God Save the Queen'. That meant everybody had to stop talking and stand still or suffer the consequences. The soldiers and police had to stand to attention. When the singing stopped everybody went home having seen once again the impossibility of having a reasoned discussion with people who, however crude and undisciplined they were, had a strange and inexplicable power to hold military, police, churches, governments and business people to ransom.

PACE still survives, most of its founder members forgotten, bringing some Catholics and Protestants together and frustrated by having them split apart again by the same people as before.

I slipped away from it after a few years, when it was well on its way.

PACE was an experiment by people who wanted change, but most of whom did not want a lot of it. Jimmy Scott wanted radical change and it was a sad loss when he died in December 1970. He did not live to see a cure but he did live to see the bursting of a political abscess.

In that month's PACE journal I tried to suggest an ideal we could share. Antagonisms were being carefully nurtured and richly rewarded in our community but still there were opportunities for development.

> When thinking about solutions to the problem of Community Relations in Northern Ireland, one is tempted to think first of all about some kind of physical mixing of Protestants and Catholics. For example, they should be integrated into one school, or into one housing estate, or into discussion groups and social and cultural associations.

> Many are now thinking in rather different terms. Part of the

reason for people's unwillingness to come together is that they feel they have nothing to offer each other. They feel that their position is being threatened and what little they have may be taken from them. There is as much a crisis of self confidence in Northern Ireland today as a crisis of authority.

We have to raise the morale of areas in Northern Ireland which are not only economically but mentally and spiritually depressed.

The first stepping stone to better Community Relations is the development of communities which are accepted at their own evaluation. If a group of people think of themselves as totally Protestant then they should be accepted as such; another group which thinks of itself as totally Catholic should be accepted as such. To say this may well raise cries of horror, but it is, one may well believe, a temporary measure. The result should be a raising of the morale of the district, a new conviction on the part of the people that they are able to manage their own affairs very much better than they thought, and a feeling that at last they have something to offer. They cease to be afraid either of themselves or of others.

In such community development one must begin with what people are able to do best, whether it is arranging social functions or forming a new company. Such is the depressed state of many of our city areas in Northern Ireland that morale must be raised on many fronts. It is a constant surprise to those who go into a depressed area from a relatively prosperous one that there is such a lack of facilities and an almost complete absence of those associations and activities which in any normal community serve to bring out the best talent and initiative of the people.

The control of community associations and community activities must pass from the traditional Church Hall to the Community Centres which will be controlled entirely by the people at large. This may in the short term seem to be a loss for the Churches but in the long term can do nothing but good. There will have to be programmes of adult education far more imaginative and stimulating than anything we have known in the past. Plays, films, the printed word will have to be used to stimulate interest in more formal adult education classes and promote initiative.

The end product of this process must be a demand by the people for increased employment opportunities. It may mean also the initiation of enterprises by the community as such. This would represent a more radical change than perhaps appears at first sight. Co-operatives have been begun in country areas with a good deal of success, but the thinking behind them has not yet been applied to city areas. There seems no real reason why it should not be.

In any such development of course the provision of small capital will be essential and is needed from public funds and from voluntary organisations. The underlying ideal which supports this kind of thinking is that the newly regained self confidence of people and hence their ability to work constructively must lead in the short term to the improvement of their own area and in the long run to their willingness to share with others. It is difficult to imagine a new and profitable co-operative or other community enterprise going on in the Falls Road which would not attract the attention and co-operation of others who, whatever their differences in religion and culture, share the common human aim of making as much money as possible.

The key to the matter is that community enterprise can raise the depression of demoralised areas and even induce prosperity. Private enterprise has been tried. Now community enterprise should be given a trial as well.

How acceptable is this kind of thinking? It is generally recognised that public authorities have not the complete answer to any problem of community. It will be necessary for people as a whole to take some part in attracting work to depressed areas. Apart from any other consideration, the political implications of a decision to site industry anywhere are so great that while one section of a community gets lazy through presuming that the party will look after them, another gets apathetic from knowing it won't. It is, at very least, easier to bring work if the people of any area are desperately anxious to attract it and have shown by the success of their own small enterprises that they are capable of doing it.

There are of course some who fear that allowing too much initiative to be taken by the people in depressed areas will lead to loss of control. It probably will, that is to say it will lead to the loss of paralysing control which was exercised in the past and will lead to a new distribution of control –or of power, if that is what one means in effect. One has to face the dilemma. The end of such thinking on community development means some change in political thinking as well. But it is a more acceptable way of reaching a new kind of society than beating each other over the head.

And it has one obvious advantage. Whereas beating each other over the head does not lead to better relations all round, this kind of thinking probably would. There is nothing helps integration so much as both sides wanting to show off their achievements.

Into our mix of hope and opposition to hope in the sixties the civil rights movement appeared, was resisted and was driven off the streets.

When people stopped asking favours and demanded rights, we did not appreciate how violent the opposition would be but just before the attacks on Belfast Catholics in August 1969 we knew something violent was going to happen to us. It had happened often before. So, knowing it was going to happen again, people went around arranging shelter for the inevitable stream of refugees who would be burned and shot out of their homes. They asked for the schools to be opened. This was for the school management committees to decide but people were in no mood for niceties. Their message was quiet and clear, that when the emergency occurred, the schools and halls would be opened with or without permission.

The pogroms came, as they always did when our coming together became inconvenient for the regime, and thousands of refugees, men, women and children, streamed into our area. The public authorities broke down; the police were among the attackers; the Red Cross was an embarrassment, concerned first with the control of money and second with preventing people using the red cross symbol for safety as they drove their pathetic loads of furniture across town, risking stones and bullets in doing it.

The refugees from 1969 onwards were invited into homes, school halls and classrooms. Babies had to be provided for, children, women and men had to sleep with the misery of fleeing from their homes. Men and women now facing days and nights without sleep were grateful for cigarettes which were considered more respectable then than now. Whether the school managers or public authorities liked it or not the buildings were made into refugee centres and local people took care of those whom the public authorities could not or would not yet take responsibility for. In West Belfast, one of the areas of greatest poverty in the city, homes, many of which were already full to capacity, opened their doors to whoever needed to come in. Food was provided by people who often had little enough for themselves. Everybody was given shelter, a feat which governments did not even attempt. Food was not always provided by families. Sometimes vans and lorries were hijacked too and their contents distributed. None of us made any objection to that; merchants could recoup their losses; refugees could not afford even to have any.

As far as most of us were concerned all we could do was ask how we could help and then do the best we could. Organisation was not created, it happened. It was summer holiday time and schools were vacant, but whatever time of year it was they would have been opened to the refugees anyway.

People formed welfare committees in the district, citizens' defence committees too who put up barricades and stood behind them day and night with little to offer in defence against invaders apart from sticks, stones, petrol bombs and eventually a trickle of firearms. As the smell of burning houses once again invaded our noses and the anger rose, very few of us raised academic moral questions about the right of people to resist by whatever means were available. People not only had the right to defend themselves, they had a duty as well. The question was, how?

We saw with anger and horror the destruction in Bombay Street and many other streets in 1969. Bombay Street became a symbol of what was happening to people and what people were prepared to do about it. The street would one day be rebuilt not only as a dwelling place but as a symbol of courage and the determination to survive with dignity.

It survived to be attacked again even into the first years of the twenty first century. Walking along that street and other burned out streets in 1969 I felt the anger welling up in me. It meant the death of the sixties' hopes. The stink of burned-out buildings, the raped homes, the religious and family pictures still clinging to what was left of the walls, remembering the efforts made to create friendship with all our neighbours, we saw once again how cruelly people were destroyed when the time came for the secret societies and government to reassert their dominance.

I walked along the devastated street with Sydney Callaghan, a Methodist minister, one of our friends. The BBC filmed us walking together and making our comments. My anger was not lessened by what followed.

The BBC filmed Sydney and myself as we talked. They arranged to broadcast the film along with a studio discussion between Cardinal Conway, Archbishop George Otto Simms, Eric Gallagher and the Presbyterian Moderator, chaired by Malcolm Muggeridge. Sydney Callaghan and I were given a separate room in the BBC to watch the film and studio discussion as they were broadcast on a Sunday evening.

The film ran and the studio discussion began. Sydney leaned over to me and whispered, 'They're not even speaking the people's language'. Muggeridge, with the affected exasperation of the highly politicised poseur he was, asked the panel, 'Do you think anger is an appropriate response for a Christian clergyman to make to this situation?' The streets might be burning, the people in agony, but Muggeridge professed to believe the burning question was not the houses but the orthodoxy of a clergyman who said he was angry at the destruction of his neighbours.

To his credit and our gratitude Conway, although taken aback by the fatuous question, said the anger was understandable, whether Christian or not. The conversation after that was bland and went nowhere.

When the programme was over I met Muggeridge in the lift and asked him, 'Did you really expect to get anything worthwhile out of all that?' He answered, 'No, not really'. I suspected that was exactly what he was brought over from London to get.

In a few days' time the men and women looking after the refugee centres were very tired. I got a phone call from one of them, a teacher in a local school, asking if anything could be done to relieve them. We arranged to call a meeting of all the people working in the emergency centres to discuss relief, supplies, work shifts and so on. He would phone some, I would phone others. I phoned some of the centres and then was stopped short. I was told we need not bother having such a meeting because the bishop had already arranged one. This was a surprise because none of the people in the centres knew anything about it. It seemed as if the church meeting was being arranged because the workers in the centres were arranging one themselves.

It seemed easier for us all to let the bishop's meeting go ahead without comment and to leave it to them. People were exhausted and if church authorities were willing to go in and help them, why not let them? There was more than enough work for as many as were willing to do it. Those working in our area agreed to go to the church officials' meeting.

However, it soon appeared that this hastily arranged meeting had a number of purposes. One was certainly to help the refugees, but another was to control whatever was being done by anybody. Church and political leaders were nervously watching the emergence of informal welfare groups, policing groups, and who knew but there might be informal military groups as well and if local groups controlled school buildings, where would all this organising lead to?

By the time the bishop's meeting took place it was clear that the safety of the people was not the only consideration and some felt irritated by this. When the bishop arrived accompanied by some priests, I could not bring myself to offer to shake hands with him, the normal courtesy. I thought we had one purpose in all this and there was no room for politicking or plotting about taking or losing control. He asked me, 'Are you not going to shake hands with me?' I said, 'Very well, I will'. We shook hands, but both of us knew where we stood, I a small ecclesiastical person, he a powerful one surrounded by advisers who were willing to control not only events but him as well.

9

For or Against the People?

It became clear at the meeting that the bishop intended to take over the relief work. Without invitation, he occupied the chair, flanked by some clergy. It was suggested from the floor that a committee should be set up to coordinate the welfare and relief work. This was agreed. Then by a substantial majority I was elected chairman of the proposed committee. The bishop did not want this. He said he wanted another priest, Sean Lowry, to chair the committee. While the disagreement was developing between what the meeting decided and what the bishop wanted I was sitting beside Paddy Wilson, a city councillor who was later stabbed to death by loyalists, and signalled to him to come outside for a moment. I told him I did not want to be chair of the committee because there were other things I could do in the area and asked him did he think I should go back in and say so. He said, 'No; let it go. Say nothing'. We went in again and found the bishop adamant that his choice should be chair and the people just as adamant that theirs should be. A compromise was reached to have two chairmen, Sean Lowry and myself.

All this was unnecessary and irritating. People were exhausted; they wanted the relief work done; they also wanted to be heard. Power and control games and the people who run them at a time like this were a nuisance.

After the meeting, or perhaps before it was over, I drove to my family's home, leaving the elected committee to get on with what was going to be directed by the bishop, not by the people. I could have said there and then that I did not consent to be either chairman or co-chairman and ask the people to be content with Sean Lowry as chairman. But I did not want either to ride over people's decisions or suggest that in case of conflict they should give in to bishops. The people had reached the compromise and voted, however reluctantly, for a second chairman to sit along with their own choice, and that had to be respected.

I had great respect for Sean Lowry, who had been a student in the College while I was on the staff and had studied social policy and practice at university. There was no doubt about his ability and honesty. If Philbin had proposed him to the people as a member of their committee, I had no doubt that he would have been elected and I would have voted for him, and in a short time he would have become chairman anyway. He knew his business and I wanted to stay away from management; there were other things to do and so we could all have worked together respecting each other's dignity and abilities. High church officials tended not to take the most discreet way of doing things.

I went home to wait until I stopped feeling irritated and frustrated.

In the heat of this emergency local people had to take a hand in their own welfare, their own security, their own organising. They did but very soon there began a slow, grinding process of putting all these things back where the officials believed they ought to be, in the hands of church and state.

Later as church people took over one initiative after another each takeover was a new revelation of church officialdom using worn out methods in a world they did not realise was changing. Welfare work was taken over, defence committees were taken over, so were some of the community and youth organisations which emerged from the smoke and fire. Money of course was taken over too.

I was not long at home until I got a phone call from Fr Eamon McEnaney, bursar of Trench House, the teachers' training college, which had been allocated by the bishop as headquarters of the new central relief committee. He asked me to come to the College and help to start the work of the committee. He was a close friend, one of the four who had driven up to my relief in my first job in a lonely parochial house in 1949, but I told him I did not want to; the committee had work to do and I preferred that they go ahead with it and I would call in with him tomorrow. But, he said, 'They aren't going ahead unless you come over'.

I could understand why. I went over against my inclination and with the same foreboding I always felt when taking part in anything with a hidden agenda. The committee started work that evening. And from that day on I believe I never got a document or communication of importance as joint chairman of the committee. After some weeks I gradually slipped away from it. Other things I wanted to do could be done without church bureaucracy looking to control it. And real relief work could not have been in better hands than Sean Lowry's.

His job was to co-ordinate the relief work with all the knowledge and expertise he had. He knew what people in need were entitled to and where the public authorities were bound by law to help. But at the same time the people in the houses, schools and streets had to work on the ground, otherwise hardship would have been much greater even than it was.

Into all the confusion and organisation and at times struggles for power there floated groups or people who wanted to help, or said they did. Some were probably government agents, people of the kind who always turn up in a crisis. One of the groups who deserve the good reputation they have in Ireland is the Quakers. I would rather call them the Society of Friends, but they seem happy being called the Quakers. Like Mother Teresa, they often have to content themselves with repairing the damage other people have done, leaving the causes of the damage untouched. They set up canteens for relatives visiting prisoners at a time when prisoners and their friends were treated by many as enemies of society. They did many other things too and would have done more if they had had the wholehearted cooperation of the Christian churches.

They wanted a corner of a field in front of Our Lady's Home in Beechmount on the Falls Road. The field was being used for grazing cows. They wanted to build a hall there for refugees living in emergency huts nearby. They said they would build the hall at their own expense so they asked if I would approach the bishop to ask him to let them lease it. I explained that my approaching him would not be the best way to get it but that was what they wanted. I asked the bishop and of course the answer to me and to them was no. So the people continued to live in their huts at Beechmount where they said the rats were as big as cats while nervously arranging their nights out in a city where it could be deadly even to go downtown. And the cows went on grazing.

The attacks on Catholic homes in August 1969 and the following years were the unionist attempt at a final solution. If Catholic church leaders had stood firm and shown sufficient anger, frustration and firm determination to protect their own people, the British government would have been forced to create some form of democracy in the northeast. It would have had to make a choice in face of the anger and clear speech of hierarchy and other influential members of the church: either give justice and democracy to the people or persecute their leaders. The London government would have been afraid to persecute the leaders of the Catholic church; it would have destabilised their politics at home as well as in Ireland. So we arrived at the situation where the British government was favouring church leaders while persecuting the church's ordinary members. Governments did this in other countries as well as Ireland.

Priests reacted variously to this situation. Some said they had their own field to plough, their own parochial or other local work to do and that was all they could do, the wider issues being a matter for the high clergy. Some protested to the bishops about their lack of effective action.

Others made their protests against government policy as best they could, but mostly without official support from their leaders. Sixty-five priests met in a Belfast hotel to protest against what the British army was doing to our people. As the years passed it became less likely that such a number of them would do such a thing again. Some Catholics were not in favour of them doing it at all. A prominent Catholic hotelier said the hotel room should not have been rented to them for such a meeting.

Later, protesting against the corruption of the judicial system, some priests refused to fill in their census forms, knowing that the public authorities would have to act against them. They were fined and said they would not pay, being prepared to go to prison. Only one of them got as far as being brought to prison and having the preliminaries for imprisonment completed. The fines of all of them were paid by someone unknown. Many believed they were paid by G.B. Newe, a Catholic who had gone to some lengths to favour the unionist people and reach accommodation with them. Some thought he went too far, but he thought long and hard as a committed and very public Catholic about what he should do. When he was about to join the Faulkner government in the seventies I could only say to him as a friend that there were dangers in doing this but we could not object to a man doing what his conscience said he should; after all that was what so many Catholics were saying at the time. He accepted the job of Minister for Community Relations in Brian Faulkner's cabinet.

Arguments about the plight of Catholics after 1969 went on inside the church as well as outside it, and it was a pity that the disagreements among clergy were not made public. It would have been healthier for the church if they had been. Clergy conferences still tended to concentrate on minor issues, of liturgy or things of that kind, while people were dying in the streets. Hierarchies may claim they are working behind the scenes but the task of the church is not just to do that but to give public witness to what they believe and what Catholics demand. One priest in deep frustration went to Bishop Philbin's house with a document of protest he had drawn up and demanded that Philbin sign it. Philbin, with a weakness which showed from time to time, signed it and this was one of the few church documents which gave a positive signal to Catholics that there could be some firmness in what church leaders were prepared to say to the government.

The events of 1969, with their disasters and their missed opportunities, raised many questions about how to mobilise the genius of a church against bad government and cruelty. Why was there no word from the Vatican about what was happening to us? We belonged to this international, rich and powerful institution, the Catholic church, and the Vatican seemed not to want to say anything significant about it. We wondered how so many Irish people had been burned out, killed, insulted because of the Pope and their allegiance to him and now the Pope was nowhere to be heard when these people were under attack again. The Osservatore Romano kept an undignified silence about the reasons.

There were simpler questions too. Why could we not create a factory in West Belfast, when one single Sunday could bring in the money for it? And why could we not have the most advanced and imaginative adult education project in the world? Why could we not use our international connections to overcome the attacks fomented against us by a minority within a minority in Ireland and Britain?

When we asked Trocaire to help us relieve the poverty of our people in West Belfast the answer was No. When we had a theatre of our own, one of the targets of our fun was the people who would do anything for good causes provided they were far enough away: 'We're always a snip for good causes, as long as they're far, far away'.

Because we were a church reduced almost to silence we had to find answers to the questions for ourselves.

The refugees needed money; they had lost homes and furniture, food and much else, some of them for the second or even third time. Bruce Kent, an English priest and good friend, one time chaplain in the British navy, later to become leader of the Campaign For Nuclear Disarmament, and who marched on Downing Street to demand a fair deal for Irish people living in the North, suggested we should ask the German churches for help. They were very rich from church taxes imposed by the government. We did not like that system but it brought in the money for the German churches. Being rich, they might respond to pleas for money to help our refugees. Bruce arranged a visit to Bonn.

A small group of us went over, Bruce Kent, Brian Walker and myself. We went to Bonn and explained our situation to a formidable panel of representatives of the churches. We explained carefully and at length. We were tired; it was shortly after the 1969 disaster and the interviews went on and on. Towards evening, as we drooped over the table, we were told we would break for a meal. I was glad and looked forward to bed; then we were told that after the meal we would come back for another session. The problem seemed to be, as one of our amiable interviewers pointed out to us, that they had a number of funds, one for missions, one for development and one for what sounded like 'catastrofs' – and we seemed not to fall under any of these headings. Bruce leaned over to me and whispered, 'We are just a slow burning catastrof.'

I said to him, 'This is hopeless; we'll get nothing'. He answered, 'No, be patient; we'll get there yet'.

And so we did. They gave us a substantial amount of money and promised more to come. Brian and I went back to Belfast delighted, stopping off in London to say goodbye to Bruce and also to go and see, for what reason I cannot understand, 'Clockwork Orange'. This film had been withdrawn from circulation at some stage and was one of the most ghastly films I ever saw, probably the turning point at which I finally lost that innocence which looks on films as entertainment.

But our delight was short-lived. Once home we set up a committee to administer the money promised from Germany, a committee we made as broad as we could. Then we got word that the German church people had been told that if any money was coming into Ireland from German churches it must be given officially through the local Irish churches. We did not understand why it should be necessary for local churches to control this money. In time to come they would make the excuse that they did not want money to get into the hands of what they called at that time 'paramilitaries' but were later to call – somewhat gleefully I thought – 'terrorists'. Our committee was as far from being terrorists as could be imagined. And anyway they did not consult us.

I never knew what happened the money, who got it or what they did with it.

10

Interval with Soldiers

Sometimes, even in the worst of times, in the nineteen seventies and eighties, British soldiers in the streets would tell us they were Catholics too. They seemed to think it would make them acceptable. Somewhere in Britain there was a mock-up village where they were trained and led to believe that the trouble in Ireland was not their bad government in London but our bad people around our own doors. They were trained to act accordingly, to view us with suspicion, antagonism and if necessary hatred. It was not necessarily their natural way of behaving; it was due to their carefully engineered training. So when the British Parachute crowd arrived in our district in 1970 they already had a vocabulary of anti-Catholic and anti-Irish hatred. When they beat three of us with their rifle butts in Springhill they asked no questions, demanded no identification, just attacked us in the street. One of the men with me said I was a priest and after a few moments the beating stopped. But the foul-mouthed anti-Catholic and anti-Irish abuse which had been going on during the beating did not stop. I had lived in Belfast all my life and had never experienced such a torrent of vile verbal abuse as this. They were only a few hours in Belfast but clearly they had been supplied with a vocabulary of abuse before they left home, wherever home was.

They went up and down the streets of our district and shouted after the women, 'fenian whores' and worse. None of us could do anything about that; they had the power, money, guns in their hands and governments and churches behind them. I still feel a deep anger that we who belonged to one of the most powerful, influential and learned institutions in the world should be so abused while the leaders and other rich beneficiaries of our church should never lift a finger to help. As we heard story after story of physical and verbal government sponsored abuse we remembered what Jesus Christ said – He had them well summed up: 'You bind burdens for people's backs and never lift a finger to move them'. Many people who stayed with the churches even when their leaders became materialistic walked away when their soldiers shouted 'fenian whores' at them in the poor streets and there was no cry of outrage from the rich ones.

The soldiers, Catholics or other, were professional killers who took pride in their profession. Courtesy in personal meetings with any of them was all right if they were willing for it but we did not expect to change them by it. In the early nineteen seventies British soldiers could go into shops or even into church for Sunday Mass if they were so inclined. A newsagent on the Falls Road described those who came into her shop. Soldiers bought comics. Men armed with deadly weapons. That they came in to buy comics was alarming enough but what really appalled her was that the comics they bought were for pre-teenagers. It was easy to understand why they had to be given cards explaining when they could fire shots. They had been trained to do what they were bidden to do, but not to think. They depended on their officers rather than their own abilities to keep them safe and bring them back from Ireland alive.

All reports to church officials about the danger of allowing such men – and later women – free range in a crowded city went unheeded. Men of the quality of Frank Cahill, who worked for church and community during those years and until his death in the nineteen nineties, pleaded in vain for church people to understand what was happening to our neighbours. But prejudice among many fellow Catholics as well as others was too deep to be rooted out just because suffering people said it should. In the decades after 1969 the people often created events, conferences, exhibitions, talks, discussions, meetings, public inquiries to show what was really happening to them and these were received with scepticism or ignored by many who could have helped.

When they beat us up in Springhill Avenue we decided not to say anything in public about it. Four of us were returning to the House after leaving some elderly people home when these 'paratroopers' leaped out at us. Our situation in the nineteen seventies was inflamed enough; we did not want to inflame it further by saying they attacked a priest and his fellow workers because in any dispute between the people of Springhill and the British soldiery, the soldiery at that time would win. In the long run they would lose but that was a long way ahead.

Not only had these soldiers the weapons but they were trained to hate us. Our people could not afford to confront them and lose. So we went to the Mater Hospital accident department and told them we had had an accident, saying nothing about soldiers who beat us on our backs with rifle butts. The following day I watched a young man being beaten as he clung on to the church railings. I could not move down the stairs quickly enough even to shout at the soldiers doing it. We had been led to believe that if you treated governments, military and police with reason they could be reasonable in return. We gave up that idea after many trials and repeated errors. Looking back now I find it hard to think without shame how hard we tried. The notion of soldiers as peace makers or peace keepers is bizarre. I came to believe, and still believe, that to join a standing army now is immoral and those who value moral standards should say so. Arming for defence is one thing; walking into a recruiting station and offering to kill in return for the state's money cannot be justified. Churches should have no place for such mercenaries.

When the British soldiery arrived in strength in 1969 we were told they were there to protect us. Later, Harold Wilson and others admitted they came to uphold and protect the regime which was oppressing us. If we were ever protected it was a side effect of British policy, not the reason for it. From the start it was the civilians who were protecting the soldiers. The military observation posts were set on top of nurses' homes and residential tower blocks, beside schools, in residential areas where it would be impossible for anyone to attack them without being accused of attacking civilians. The civilians were protecting the soldiers, not the other way round.

My brother Liam pointed this out to me in the early seventies when I was too naive to notice it myself. The Grand Central Hotel stood in the centre of Belfast, at one time the poshest hotel in town. The British army took it over and with startling inability to assess even their own situation, arranged a presentation of shamrock to the troops by a member of their royal family on the first St Patrick's Day after their occupation. There came a time when they could not even venture out the door without heavy armour and blackened faces but at the beginning they put on the same show as they put on for inhabitants of so many countries, the power and the glory expressed in symbols borrowed from the natives and often protected by them. It was also my brother Liam who remarked to me the strange irony that the British governor in Hillsborough was the only man in the country who needed to stick feathers in his hat to make him look important. The empire builders were dying away still clutching their fading symbols

Soldiers felt secure in the Grand Central because encircling a wide area around the hotel there were security gates, heavy metal barriers, turnstiles, all staffed by civilians. Before getting as far as the British military headquarters in the Grand Central you had to be searched and passed by civilians.

The protection civilians gave the soldiers took many forms: the creation of these civilian search points, soldiers arming civilians to fight their undercover battles for them, civilian organisations infiltrated by agents subverting and gathering information for them. For British army officers the main task, as they admitted, was to go back home with all their soldiers still alive. With all the protection they got from armour, arms and civilian guard posts it was remarkable they lost any. They finally admitted that the armed republicans were a dedicated, competent and formidable military force whom they could not defeat, even with all their civilian and military protection. But they tried hard.

When great numbers of British troops came on to our streets in 1969 most of us were very naive. British troops had never been out of the place but after 1969, instead of keeping a discreet distance, they crowded our streets. Up to that time some girls still married British troops, and even after the attempted final solution of 1969 some still went to British army barracks for dances or socials. Even during the early seventies some girls married British soldiers but as time went on they went over to England to do it. The official propaganda at the time said our hatred of each other was the cause of what was happening in Ireland. This was false. People were angry at bad government, bullying and insult and it was right they should be, but the ties between all of us in Ireland and Britain were too close for us to hate each other just because of what we were. Our ties with fellow members of our community in Belfast made indignation possible but hate for most of us almost impossible. Hate was a carefully cultivated interest among a too powerful minority.

Because we had been trying, especially in the fifties and sixties, to come together in cooperation with Protestant clergy, we naturally accepted chaplains who came in with the British army as clergymen rather than soldiers. We were too naive to heed the warnings of writers like Gordon Zahn (Gordon C. Zahn, Chaplains in the RAF) who said bluntly that priests in an army are soldiers first and priests afterwards. We were willing to think the best of them rather than the worst.

While British army officers could still go to Mass in Ballymurphy for a time after August 1969, Catholic and Protestant army chaplains were welcomed into people's homes because they were clergy. Looking back on it we can be proud of naiveté of this kind; it was what we understood by hospitality. Sometimes local clergy would go out for a meal with chaplains. We trusted each other, or thought we did. Catholic or Protestant clerics we considered non-combatants. The People's Theatre invited the chaplains to a performance in the local school hall of 'The Soldiers' Synge', in which we mocked their officers. They asked for the play to come to the local barracks; the cast politely declined the invitation. As time went on we realised they were not non-combatants. People began to complain that when received courteously into houses the chaplains asked questions which 'only police and soldiers would ask'; some of them went around with their firearms showing. One of the Catholic chaplains went to a local pub, fraternised with the people and asked questions which suggested he was gathering information.

A Catholic priest, especially in hard times, depends on people trusting him. Once that trust goes he might as well pack up and go. If people trust him it matters little what armies and governments say about him, but once his neighbours' trust in him goes, then even if he were a saint and a scholar, his work is ruined. That is one of the reasons why we were angry when we found they were gathering information for their army authorities. I asked a senior chaplain whether one of them, Gerry Weston, had done this voluntarily or been got at by the army. Without hesitation he replied: ' I think he was got at.'

Thinking this should be put on record to alert people and make the British government realise this tactic was no longer of use to them, I sent a letter to the Catholic Standard. I was writing a column for it at the time and the letter would probably be published whereas in a bigger paper it might not, and the important thing was to have it down on the record, then it could filter through to more and more people without causing a major public row. Why we wanted to avoid a major public row is hard to understand without understanding the way we thought at the time. Why not report the matter to the church authorities? Few of us would have presumed the church authorities would be on our side in such a matter. The more likely response would be to tell us all to keep quiet about it.

But filtering the thing through to public consciousness did not work. The paper's editor, John Feeney, whose thoughts about it were less delicate than ours, did not publish the letter as a letter; he put it on the front page of the paper. I had told him he could use it any way he liked. Then the trouble began again: publication in other papers, recriminations, denials and so forth. The Catholic bishop for the British Army, Bishop Tickle, made a unique visit to Belfast to say such things did not happen. His press conference was an embarrassment even to the British army press officer who had to guide him through it and eventually rescue him from it. The fact remained that chaplains had been engaged in information gathering by using their position as clergy and that was wrong. Whatever arguments might be put up by those in authority, the trust between priests and neighbours would be wrecked if we knew this was happening and did nothing about it. Decades later, when other scandals in the church were hidden by those in authority the loss of trust was disastrous.

The chaplains were told by their authorities to back off and that was the end of the socialising and invitations to take part in worship or theatre. Naiveté, hospitality and trying to love your military fellow Christians can be a dangerous mix.

By chance Fr Gerry Weston, the most active information-gatherer, was the priest killed by the Official IRA bomb in Aldershot a few years later.

When the big attacks started in 1969, the Moral Rearmament people arrived in our district. They identified community leaders and some of these who in the past had great difficulty getting anybody to notice them were now approached and offered attractive things to do. They might be offered a course of leadership training, or a few weeks holiday away from home. Moral Rearmament seemed not to have any plans for good government, which was our basic aim, or to create factories, which we were trying to do. It seemed they were content to help people change their minds.

Many people told us we should change our minds. When we said the government was bad, its institutions oppressive, and we were worried, alarmed and angry about this, we were told: 'If you adjust your mind you can come to terms with all this and so your problem will be solved'. But our intention was not to adjust our minds and come to terms with it but to change it. Good-doing organisations, including some church and peace groups, were giving us the same message.

In 1976 Fr Frank Culhane invited me to go to Switzerland, where he was chaplain to the English-speaking community in Lausanne. I knew he wanted to offer me a holiday with a good excuse for being away and little to do while I was there. I was working on a dissertation about community education and it was a good opportunity to get on with it. While I was in Lausanne a friend, Father Fox, came one day and asked if I would like to visit the Moral Rearmament place up in the mountains. Of course I would, and off we went. It was up the mountains right enough but was much more than just a place – an enormous palace clinging to the mountainside approached by a quaint railway. The size and magnificence of it were breathtaking.

Inside the palace people in attractive dresses, people in long robes, in ordinary suits, Europeans, Americans, Indians went around the great wide corridors. Those corridors seemed each as wide as the whole ground floor of our house in Belfast. This had once been a hotel for extremely rich people visiting Switzerland for the skiing. It still had all the appearance of wealth and splendour now that it was owned by the Moral Rearmament people. There was a lot of money in there somewhere.

A meeting was going on in one of the large rooms and I said 'yes' when invited to sit in at it. At first it was difficult to understand what it was about, but gradually it became clear. On the long deep dais there were, among others, two families, fathers, mothers, two children each. They were from Liverpool and Birkenhead. They were talking – giving witness, someone told me. The father of one of the families told how he had intervened in a dockers' strike and had, as he said, succeeded in persuading the dockers to go back to work. This was greeted with applause and the other father had a message of much the same kind, to more applause. I did not wait for the whole session as we had to go back to Lausanne. But I had heard enough to realise that what was being applauded here was working people who had helped to break strikes which for all I knew might well have been fully justified for better wages and conditions. The wages and conditions were not being discussed; the ending of the strike was. It seemed like getting rid of trouble not by changing conditions but by aiming at the potential trouble makers and neutralising them. Like the Peace People and other peace groups later on, what was desired was peace without substantial political or economic change. For those of us who believed that peace could only come through substantial change it was revelatory and explained why the Moral Rearmament people arrived so quickly and so well equipped when trouble came, when hitherto quiet people went out protesting on the streets.

After 1969 our neighbours had their choice: they could treat everyone as a possible spy, an official or unofficial information gatherer or a counter-revolutionary of some kind, but that would be against the grain and would drive away people who sincerely wanted to help. When visitors came we described our situation without naming names. We even had what we came to call cultivated forgetfulness. You did not ask people's names if they did not give them. If you did know, or get to know their names you sometimes purposely forgot them. Ever since the British soldiers came into our house and went through my files I did not put much on paper. When I asked them if they would go into the house of an Anglican priest in England and search what might well be private papers about private people, and what would happen them if they did, they hesitated and stopped. I took whatever papers I had away to a safe place after that and put things on paper as little as possible, keeping as little information in my head as necessary. Many of our neighbours were tortured for information. Any of us could break down if we were tortured and anybody could be tortured, some of the most uninvolved of our neighbours were. What you do not know you cannot say, even if they did abuse you. To say nothing, the best way is to know nothing and hence came cultivated forgetfulness. You keep things in your head as long as you need them, then forget them.

When the war was over we had to try to restore our memories which had been so damaged.

Part of the government's tactics was to make us believe we were always being watched; big brother could see and hear everything. Their spying technology was expensive and sophisticated but you cannot defeat determined people by technology. You may hurt them but you cannot defeat them. People with little modern technology can still do remarkable things against the wishes of a government.

Infiltration of people's associations by government agents was often tried and often worked. Among the Protestant population there were political organisations of three kinds, those which had arisen in answer to conditions on the ground, those which had started this way and been infiltrated by British government agents, military or police, and those which had been set up by British spy services from the start. I thought that of those we were interested in the UDA was among the second of these and the Red Hand Commando among the third. There were few organisations among Protestant working people which had not been either specially set up or infiltrated and while republican military groups reorganised from time to time to counter such infiltration, the Protestant based groups seemed never able or willing to do that effectively. The republicans had long experience of resistance to state authorities while Protestant groups could only with difficulty understand that state authorities were not on their side either. They began by trusting the military and police and continued to do so even long after the British government made it plain that they too were expendable. John McKeague of the Red Hand Commando told us his moment of truth came in Long Kesh. He was interned without trial and when a British officer with his batman approached him in the camp, John appeared along with his batman too and treated the officer as an equal. After all he too was a soldier working for British Ulster. The British officer knocked him down with his fist. But many of his fellow loyalists continued to trust the British forces long after it was clear that their trust was not returned. Their bitter resentment and frustration against the government was often worked out not against the government forces but against the Catholics. Not always however.

One day a woman came to our house, recommended to us by a city councillor. She told us she was doing a thesis for an English university. She asked about the situation in Belfast and we talked to her with the usual safety precautions. She wanted to stay in our neighbourhood and we arranged for her to lodge in a house in the estate. We asked her if she would like to talk to people 'on the other side', people belonging to Protestant associations. We always did that, and sometimes the compliment was returned. We had our story, they had theirs and anyone was entitled to hear them all. So we got in touch with friends in a loyalist area and arranged for her to call over and visit them.

Soon after she went over a phone call came to us from our loyalist friends. 'Do you know who that woman is that you sent over?' 'We understood she is doing a sociology thesis for a university.' 'She's policewoman.' 'She's what?' 'A policewoman. She told us. And we have told her she will never again abuse the hospitality of anybody in this city the way she abused the hospitality of your people over there. She cannot go back there in any circumstances and we have told her so. She can stay with us if she wishes but she will not go back to your neighbourhood unless she tells people exactly who she is.' 'Agreed. Will you meet us half way and we'll bring her bags from the house she was in?' 'No. Come over here and bring her bags with you. She will see how the land lies.' So I took her bags from the house where she had been staying, making some excuse to the people there, who have not been told yet what really happened, because they would be embarrassed. In the house of our loyalist friends the policewoman was sitting forlorn in the sitting room as they told her once again that she would not abuse the hospitality of anyone in this city and expect approval from them because they were loyalists. I bade them all goodbye, thanked our friends for their courtesy and went home.

11

Goodbye Sisters

After the massive inflow of British troops into the north of Ireland in 1969 and 1970, some clergy felt not only nervous but ashamed. The military had come on the streets in large numbers to help the police contain what they saw as a revolution. Christians in Belfast prided themselves on being the most church-going people in Europe and in no need of force to keep them in order. How awful, one of them, a Methodist, said, that black soldiers should be on our streets to keep us in order, that These People had to keep us from rioting.

The black soldiers were Englishmen from Manchester or Liverpool, Scots or Welsh from Glasgow or Swansea and should have been as welcome or unwelcome as other British men and women soldiers but this did not cut any ice. They were black and we were supposed to civilise the black people, not the other way about.

One day a Methodist clergyman phoned from London asking would it be a good idea for Mother Teresa of Calcutta to come to Belfast. I said it would. She had in mind to come to Belfast and perhaps set up a house on the peace line. My blood which warmed to the idea of her coming ran cold. If Teresa came and set up a house on the peace line it would reinforce the idea that our problems were the result of inter-faith conflict rather than bad government and this would be damaging. When I seemed hesitant he asked whether I thought the idea of her coming would not be a good one after all. No, the possibility of her coming was too good to miss. I suggested she should come on a visit, come to our area, see for herself, talk to people, make up her own mind about what she should do. If I were asked I would say, 'Don't set up a religious house on any peace line but look at the real reasons for our political, religious and economic problems and then decide what to do'.

It was arranged that she would come on a visit to Belfast, would come to our parish, attend Mass in Corpus Christi church in Ballymurphy and decide for herself what she should do afterwards. Her visit would be good, not least because there had been so much unfair propaganda about West Belfast and Ballymurphy. Part of the benefit of Mother Teresa's visit was that her Sisters wanted to come into Ballymurphy rather than flee from it – that would confound the hostile press and confuse those who had tried to make a derelict ghetto of it. So let her come, and welcome. The work her Sisters would do would be foremost of course, but there were these other benefits as well.

The welcome Teresa got was greater than any of us expected. Our Presbyterian and Quaker friends and others were very happy at the visit. So Teresa came, sat in the sanctuary during the Mass which I had the honour of celebrating. When I introduced her to the congregation who knew so well already who she was, they applauded her and made her welcome there and then. Some of us had been wondering what we should do after the Mass; should we bring her around here or there or wherever, and what would she want to see? It was all unnecessary. Once the Mass was over the people took her in hand, gathered around her, gave her personal welcomes to go with the formal welcome she had already got. Then she disappeared.

None of us knew where she went. But she was in good hands; we knew that, even if we did not see her for a while. When she returned she was radiant. The neighbours had shown her around and talked to her while she in her usual way talked to them only a little but affectionately. By the time the tour was over she had made up her mind what to do. In the afternoon she went to visit Bishop Philbin. To the surprise of most of us she came back into the district with the news that he had said 'yes' to her suggestion that her Sisters set up house in Ballymurphy. We could hardly believe our good fortune and our view of the bishop brightened.

Other visits had been arranged for Teresa and her companion in Belfast and they were welcomed wherever she went. It was a nice scene of cooperation between Protestants, Catholics and others in a city where propaganda said such cooperation could not happen.

The Springhill house I was renting was still being prepared at this time and in order to get Teresa's nuns in as soon as possible – that is what they wanted and so did we – we arranged for the Sisters to get the house that had been allocated to me and I would get another one later which the Housing Executive would make ready as soon as possible. The Sisters got two houses, one to live and pray in, the other to work and pray in. They put up a notice outside their dwelling house saying 'Missionary Sisters'. The men and women of the neighbourhood cooperated with our friends from outside and in a short time the Sisters had whatever they needed. Their needs were few, too few and too small for some people who wanted them to live more comfortably than they wanted to themselves.

We did not realise that the plaque outside their door announcing they were 'Missionary Sisters' would cause them and us considerable pain.

When they put up their plaque the word 'missionaries' made some people uncomfortable. We send missionaries to India; they do not send them to us. Perceptive Christians like Tomás Ó Fiaich realised that this is exactly what was likely to happen in the future when clergy and religious would come from Africa or India or wherever because our church could no longer supply enough of its own.

In spite of the welcome they got, Mother Teresa's sisters had to leave Belfast but it was not by their own choice, and we tried to keep them. There was an underlying racism among some influential high clergy, and of these a few talked of foreign religious in terms of one-meal curries and not-too-demanding hygiene. When we realised the Sisters were being told they were not needed and therefore not wanted we thought the sensible thing was to make known publicly just how good they were, how cultivated and well qualified. It seemed the only way to keep them.

One of the Sisters came into our house and said she would be glad of our prayers for her sister at home in Delhi. I thought her sister was ill but, no, she was just about to complete her studies for a doctorate in music. This was a far cry from the muttered 'What could they teach our people?' which we had heard from a few, fortunately few, clergy who should have known better or if they did not know better should have had the wit to keep their ideas to themselves.

We suggested to the Sisters that while we admired their completely self-effacing way of life, it would be important to make their qualifications known to avoid the Sisters being undervalued. One of them had post-graduate qualifications in nursing, another had recently done a course of theology in Rome, which was more than any of us clergy had been doing. We suggested we should make known through the media just what kind of people they were and what qualifications, as well as qualities they brought with them. But they would have none of it. Because we were insistent, they agreed to consult Teresa about it. We all knew what she would say and she said it. Their approach to people was founded on the respect they had for them, offering a simple declaration of regard rather than certificates of qualification. She did not put it exactly like that but that is what she meant. The Sisters and those working with them could approach people with both, and there were times when qualifications had to be shown, but she did not see the matter in the same way as we did. We knew the game was up and the Sisters would go. When the Sister was asking for prayers for her sister's doctorate, she hinted as much.

The annual parish pilgrimage was shortly to go to Lourdes, organised by a dedicated and hard working fellow curate. Before we left for Lourdes the Sisters said they would probably be gone when we came back. There was little we could do. We could appeal to Teresa, but the Sisters would stand by what she said and not try to persuade her one way or another.

I would have liked to talk to her when she came to Belfast to arrange their departure but the parish group would be in San Sebastian while she was in Belfast, so I arranged to phone her from there. I did that but it was no use. She was adamant and there was justice in what she was saying. Why should the Sisters stay in Belfast where they were now made officially unwelcome when there were thirty or forty dioceses asking for them? The only plea I could make was that the Sisters should stay for another six months. I made every argument I could for that. One of the arguments coming into my head surprised me. I said if she brought the Sisters out now the church hierarchy would be blamed for it and this would damage relations between the senior clergy and the people even more.

It was a strange plea for me to make, but we had to try everything. Teresa was unmoveable. Her Sisters were going and they were going now. Our neighbours all wanted them to stay, but Teresa, while she had a spirit of enterprise and independence, was supportive of church authorities and believed the voice of God was somewhere in there behind their sometimes hard facade. In a crisis the church authorities had the right to be obeyed, whatever she or any of us might think.

When we arrived home from Lourdes the Sisters were gone.

However, not without some indication of what it cost them and us.

Before leaving Teresa started to write a letter to the bishop telling him of her dismay, frustration and indignation at what had happened. While she was doing this, word came from the bishop that she would be expected not to say anything that would reflect on the actions of the church authorities. So Teresa tore up the letter and threw it in the wastepaper basket.

By one of the strange quirks of fate that make life more interesting and hopeful one of the neighbours who had volunteered to re-arrange the Sisters' house for the next occupants found the fragments of the letter in the basket and recognised Teresa's handwriting. She thought they would make a pleasant memento of the woman whom she and her neighbours so much admired. She put the fragments together. And so was preserved a partial account of the indignant sentiments of Teresa on leaving Belfast. However, when the reconstituted letter was given to an Irish nun who had also been working in the district, she guarded it so carefully that none of us ever saw it again after she also was asked to leave. It still exists and one hopes it will continue to exist but in any case what is beyond question is that Bishop Philbin, who had been good enough to consent to Mother Teresa's Sisters coming in, was not, unfortunately, strong enough to keep them there.

Mother Teresa's visit to Belfast made us realise once more the deep desire of people to show goodwill, a desire which church people often misunderstood and undervalued.

What should our attitude to Mother Teresa have been? Some years after she had come and gone Archbishop Oscar Romero was assassinated while saying Mass in Colombia. We could see the difference between the two people. Mother Teresa was content to pick up the sad pieces left by vicious political and economic systems and got the Nobel Prize, while Romero, who attacked the causes of misery as well as picking up the pieces, was shot in the head.

Teresa had critics but we appreciated anyone who came to us in peaceful respect and wanting to help when disdain for our neighbours was considered a sign of great righteousness.

The treatment Teresa got was not the first dramatic example we had of church authorities feeling the need to control the church, so we need not have been surprised.

12

Problems with the Management

For some priests, church management was creating problems. It often had to do with controlling what was there rather than creating something better, and some became uneasy. Others said it did not matter; this was the way the church worked and most of the time some good was done and little harm. But in the north of Ireland we were in a highly volatile situation and needed all the resources we could get to heal the poverty and hurt suffered by so many people, most of them Catholics. Needing resources, trying to get them and seeing them slipping away into some place we knew nothing about became more and more difficult to accept. I thought some church policies and practices were damaging to people, clergy and church. We did not use all our vast resources to relieve poverty and communal tension. We separated clergy from people in the church and kept hold of power when more and more people were becoming more and more ready and willing to take responsibility. We did not give adequate place to women and adopted the materialists' attitude to property and to people who should have been welcomed and were marginalised instead. The great potential of priests to change our society and make it more gentle was not realised. Because of the changing times and the clouds which were going to become bigger in the future I wrote to William Philbin in 1971. The letter did not ask for much change but that priests and bishops and all members of the church should be self-confident colleagues. He was displeased with it and asked me to present my observations to the Priests' Council to which I and others had been elected as priests' representatives a few years before. Among other things the letter said in the verbose style considered proper at the time:

113

[...] awareness of the existence of a problem was shown by Bishop Guyot, President of the French Episcopal Commission for the Clergy, who said:

> *'What many priests want today is that their relations with Bishops should be in a climate of mutual confidence. They want to be able to express with full frankness their hopes and difficulties, to exchange experiences, to propose possible concrete solutions, to take certain initiatives. In other words our priests do not want simply to have the duty of carrying out decisions from above; they want to take part in the working out of the pastoral task in a diocese. They want to have a presence at the evolving of the work so that they really will be able to co-operate later on ... with very great mutual generosity. The Bishop and his Priests run the risk of proceeding along parallel ways which only meet at infinity – which, as everyone knows, is from the pastoral point of view, too late!'*

That some adjustment of relationships is necessary is becoming increasingly clear. The Osservatore Romano said, in relation to present controversies: 'Soldiers in the past war obeyed the orders of their officers without knowing the strategy of the great chiefs and the tactics of their immediate superiors. Why therefore should the divine authority of the pastors of the Church not demand a similar submission in the sphere of faith and morals?'

To place those subject to authority in the church in the same category as soldiers is a way of expressing a relationship which seems unfortunate and excluded by the Vatican Council document on Priests. Recently too Archbishop O'Boyle said that those priests who did not submit to the recent ruling in Humanae Vitae 'should go and find a pope and a church of their own'. Here again, one does not question the rights of those in authority or the duties of those bound by it, but when one considers that this implies that a priest can be cut off from the work he has been doing for years, and left – as has been made clear for instance in Southwark – without means and without home if this should be considered desirable, the only parallel one can find for this is in a master-servant relationship which is no longer found in secular affairs where the right of dismissal is being more and more restricted and dismissal itself is becoming less and less punitive.

That the relationships between priests and others is in need of serious consideration and perhaps adjustment may be seen from two incidents in our own circumstances. Here a serious deterioration is evident. Some years ago it would have been considered monstrous if a priest were publicly rebuked and humiliated in front of his parishioners. It would have been considered equally monstrous for a priest to have to submit to the indignity of acquainting his people with his own faults from his own pulpit. Nowadays these things can be and have been done. Clearly then the relationship of priests to those who have authority over them cannot be presumed to be that which the Vatican Council envisaged.

Similarly, it is clearly wrong that a priest should have been – not rebuked which would have been understandable – but abused in language which a few years ago we were accustomed to exhort people not to use because it was an abuse of God's gift of speech and a grave offence against a brother in Christ. That this should be done by a Vicar General in the name of a bishop reveals the presence of standards which as a priest one finds it increasingly difficult to share and sympathise with. One finds it particularly anomalous in a world which is rapidly coming to understand that not even servants would be subjected to verbal abuse.

It may very well be that the opinion that the relationship of priests to other members of the church is not in need of consideration and possibly of adjustment, and that it is wrong to find certain elements in the relationships which suggest a lowering of the dignity of priests. The suggestion has been made that in order to find out, and possibly to avert what is potentially a very difficult and damaging situation in which we could very well lose priests whom we can ill afford to lose, a Commission of Priests should be set up to examine every aspect of the life and work of priests in our country and our diocese. This is a suggestion which may well merit serious consideration. The priests in Ireland are by no means immune from the difficulties which priests have suffered elsewhere and unless there is recognition of the fact that relationships between priests and those in authority is in some places a most grave problem which weighs heavily on the minds of many priests, we shall suffer similar losses, losses which are all the more tragic because they could have been prevented. (Full text Appendix 1)

This letter had been intended as a memo to put certain things on the record and say there could and should be changes. It was also an indication to the Bishop of discussion I would try to raise in the Council. We needed an open discussion which would enable us all to say what our views were on all important matters. He was displeased and said I should submit it to the Council. I did not want that to happen. I thought that if this letter were presented to the Priests' Council it might appear that there was simply an argument between the bishop and me. So I drew up another, more general statement for the Council in the hope that the priests who were there would raise their own concerns, the discussion would open and the bishop would realise that open discussion was indeed necessary. This statement said:

> The Vatican Council document on priests emphasised among other things the maturity and responsibility of priests as well as their dignity.
>
> However, there are certain indications that this healthy relationship of brothers in Christ working together in harmony cannot be presumed to exist already and cannot, where it does not exist already, be brought about without efforts on the part of all of us.
>
> It may be hoped that in any revision of canon law and local statutes these should begin to express a better relationship than they do at present. Some of the laws under which priests live and work do not recognise fully their maturity or their personal responsibility. Laws which are seen to be undesirable should be revised and there is a good case therefore for priests to request that this should be done and that any revision of canon law should include the outlining of a relationship between bishops and clergy which is more in keeping with the spirit of the Vatican Council's document on the matter. This relationship is that of co-operators with the father of the flock, of priests with the fatherly representative of Jesus Christ Our Lord. The relationship envisaged in the canon law is nearer to one of master and servant and does not reflect either the desirable situation or the situation as it exists when bishops and priests are in harmony with each other.
>
> One of the major problems which will face us in the future will be that of the existing relations between priests and those in authority. In these difficult times we cannot leave such important matters to chance in the hope that everything will happen as we

wish it to happen. There has not been for many years a crisis among priests similar to that which we are experiencing today. And neither in Ireland as a whole nor in this diocese are we immune from it. Priests need all the help and understanding they can be given. It is very saddening, and very frightening too, to hear the comments of priests and to realise that there is a considerable disquiet amounting to resentment being experienced in some quarters because it is felt that they are not being treated with the consideration that is their due.

Priests must be reassured that if for example they are unfortunate because of sickness or old age they will be provided for. They must be assured too that if they commit any fault they will still be treated with dignity. It is not right that a priest should be for example subjected to indignity in front of members of his parishioners, or be addressed, whatever faults he may be seen to have committed, in abusive language. And yet these things have happened among us in recent times. That they should happen is wrong. That they should pass without vigorous comment is a sign that our standard of acceptable behaviour towards each other is lower than the charity of Our Lord Jesus Christ would demand of us.

We all need to give an example of charity and justice to each other and those in authority have a special obligation to show mercy and love and justice as well as temperance and humility to all with whom they deal. Any of us can only make a personal assessment of whether we do carry out these duties or not. I think it is an unhappy fact that we have much to reproach ourselves for in so many ways. I think also that unless we seriously face the many problems of relationships with each other in this diocese as everywhere else we shall first alienate and then lose some of our priests and some of our best lay people. And it is worth remarking if an average of two priests were eventually to leave us each year this would bring us up to the percentage which in other countries we recognise as frightening and lamentable.

In matters such as this of course a personal assessment is not enough. I have requested and now I request again that a committee of priests, elected by the priests themselves, should be set up now with the task of examining how our life and work and relationships with each other conform to the standards set by the encyclicals and by the Vatican Council.

I think there is need of it and it should be done as a matter of the greatest urgency. (Full text in Appendix)

There were many questions needing answers and the Priests' Council could discuss them. I had heard them discussed many times by priests and others and believed that an elected member of the Council should put them up for discussion. Years later Bishop Willie Walsh and others did put changing relationships within the church up for discussion but by that time it was rather late. Meanwhile we did indeed see the departure of some of our most able priests and others from attachment to the church.

On my way to the Council meeting that day, depressed at the thought of it, I gave a lift to a senior cleric. I believed it was wrong to lobby; we should go to meetings, put our observations on the table and let people say what they wanted to say, so I did not tell him what I was about to say at this meeting presided over by the bishop. Without prompting from me he talked about clerical difficulties, things that were wrong and should be changed, observations which corresponded with what I was going to say.

When my item on the agenda came up for discussion at the meeting I got a surprise. I read my piece and it was then open for discussion. The first person to speak and tell the meeting, 'Father Wilson is indicating a malaise in the church which does not exist' was the senior cleric who had come with me to the meeting. Others followed him, some of them men whom I had heard reciting these very difficulties a number of times. Some of the clergy supported what I was saying, that these matters were important and at least they should be discussed. But they were a minority that day and there was clearly no possibility of any positive outcome. It was disappointing that friends who were worried about diocesan and church matters did not support such discussion and that some of them opposed it.

On our way out from the Council meeting I found myself side by side with a priest friend, one of the minority who had supported what I said. I asked him, 'Donald, did you by any chance hear the cock crow three times during that meeting?' 'No I didn't. I didn't even know they kept hens.'

During the next couple of years I brought up some matters in the Council but neither this nor the Council itself had much effect on anything.

Eventually I resigned from it but that was about a different issue. Deciding to resign from it was simple. I had been elected by priests but had never done very much in the Council, partly because the Council was not designed for making changes and partly because, although people did not believe it, I was too reticent in face of opposition. I would not be missed on the Council.

In 1974 my time on it was nearly up. When we were coming to the end of the elected representatives' term a new issue came up which made me certain I should resign from it. The Bishop through his Vicar General told us that local clergy should take control of the Citizens' Defence Committees which people had set up during the 1969 attacks. The excuse as always was that they might fall into what church administration considered 'the wrong hands'. I said, 'no', there might come a time when defence committees might feel compelled to take arms and that was a decision other people would make, not us. It was futile to expect that the presence of clergy would stop that happening if people wanted or demanded it. Such control by clergy was a crude and useless device to try to ensure it did not happen. I asked if we were prepared to be heads of committees which might feel obliged to become armed bodies. I was told that if I did not do it others would. Others did do it but the Defence Committees gradually and inevitably were reduced to making statements for the newspapers while the church administration lost all possibility of controlling them anyway.

I decided to resign from the Priests' Council after this and a few weeks before the last meeting of our term of membership. I wrote to Bishop Philbin resigning from the Council, giving him reasons why.

Church policies and procedures were so galling to some of our colleagues that they ceased working as priests but it was a pity they felt impelled to do that. I did not intend to walk away from the Catholic priesthood. I had spent fifteen years with young men who had offered to become priests and knew the intellectual and moral quality of them. From the nineteen sixties priests were resigning from priesthood, not necessarily because they disagreed with church beliefs but because they lost confidence in church policies. There must be some way to show disagreement with church policies and remain a priest if one wanted to. If men gave up working as priests so as to do something they thought more necessary, our blessing should go with them but it was a pity if they gave up priesthood because of church policies which could be changed. In my submission to the Council I had said that if our diocese lost two priests a year this would be a crisis like crises elsewhere. The bishop resented this. Eventually the departure of priests did become a problem in Ireland too but we could perhaps have done something creative about it, creating alternative policies to those which in the long run would have to be changed anyway.

Junior curates did not have much place in church government and apart from a few bits and pieces – trustee of this building, membership of that committee – the world was not going to fall apart because I resigned from any of them. I did not want the world to fall apart; I just wanted not to have to take even such small responsibility for the direction in which church policies were leading us or failing to lead us. But could you really detach yourself from policies without detaching from priesthood?

Then one day I saw what I could do. I could retire.

When I was growing up and for long afterwards priests were expected to work until they died. You could go on being a parish priest at 85 or 95. A suggestion at the Priests' Council that something should be done to create adequate retirement provision for elderly priests was met with, 'We don't want to have a lot of priests going about doing nothing', a crude statement not of the bishop's policy but of his senior advisers, some of whom seemed to believe retirement was a defeat, as it may well have been if your aim is to keep control of things. In Belfast when I was growing up old people often clung on to management of businesses; the boss maybe remained boss long enough to see his sons retire at 65 while he worked away for years after that. At times the church, instead of changing the world, adopted its standards, good, bad or indifferent and it was when it adopted the business and power world's standards that it made its biggest mistakes. Times have changed and provision is made now for retired priests. Retirement according to Catholic church law can be arranged easily, quietly, and without recrimination.

I tried it. Unfortunately the bishop believed or was persuaded that this was just an act of defiance and he acted accordingly. He never spoke to me again. I asked him to and he refused. I asked the Priests' Council to talk with me; they refused. I asked each member separately to talk with me. Some did not reply, some refused, some would have liked to but clearly did not want to go against the bishop and his senior clergy.

Instead of accepting the church law about retirement Bishop Philbin accused me of threatening to destroy the church. Correspondence followed between us which the journalist John Cooney later described as 'byzantine', all about law and rights and suchlike. He forbade me the use of churches. My duties in the parish were now nil but I was not told this, I just did not hear from the parish priest any more. Soon people noticed and commented, journalists began to look around to see what was wrong. Unable to get any conversation with the bishop or the Council I wondered if there would be any use referring the matter for arbitration to Rome. I had long ago said the Vatican apparatus of church government should be dismantled but nobody in the Vatican would know or mind about that, so it might do some good to refer the matter to them. It does not have an effective human rights procedure, so I went to a bishop friend and asked him, 'How would it be if I referred this matter to Rome?' His answer was swift and funny. 'If you do', he said, 'you will meet a Monsignor Benelli in Rome who is roughly the Roman equivalent of X.' X was one of William Philbin's chief advisors from whom, although we were long-standing acquaintances, I would receive advice which was at best patronising and at worst dismissive. The rest of the conversation with that bishop was about old times – we were ordained in Maynooth on the same day – and about one thing and another, all thought of Rome discarded.

I did write to Rome, though, to a Cardinal Wright who I understood was head of the Congregation or church government department which dealt with clergy. His reply was so disdainful, so full of self-assurance – he did not even ask me what the trouble was – that I became furious, waited a few days and wrote a letter which in effect said so. I learned later that the poor man may have been ill at the time and indeed he died not long afterwards and this was a lesson once again that if you want to say anything, say it in a way you will never regret.

A priest denied the use of churches is made to look like a criminal. People do not know what it is all about. Irish newspapers took the matter up; articles, even editorials, were written about it and so what was meant to be a quiet adjustment with dignity became a national scandal with people taking sides one way or the other. I got all the support I could possibly need from my family while my friends in the Community House and my neighbours in West Belfast could not have been better.

After retiring I did not know what I should do. I knew what I would not do: put into practice and take even the slightest responsibility for church policies which seemed at least inadequate and at worst damaging. Political, economic, social or moral change was not going to come through the churches. It took a long time to realise we need not hope to convert any of our powerful institutions; rather we had to create some means by which people could protect themselves from all of them, reducing their hold over us as much as we could. As long as churches were humanly motivated and humanly inspired they too were unconvertible, as much so as banks, and military and big business. But people were protectable and that was the challenge they could maybe help to meet in however small a way.

Long before 1975 I had got to know the work of Dorothy Eagleson who advised people about careers. She was one of the few women in my student days who studied Scholastic Philosophy in Queen's. She was notable in a lecture room where many of the students were clerics, and all, apart from herself, men. She became head of an advisory body to help people discover the job they were best at and tell them how to get it.

So here I was with no official function in the church any more, a priest on hold who had retired but said that if church policies changed he would ask to be allowed to start again. I had no income from the church from 1975 until after the year 2000. I had to earn something. I applied for adult teaching in the prisons believing they would not accept me. They didn't. So why not consult Dorothy Eagleson as we had all recommended others to do in the past?

I went, we talked, she gave me a questionnaire to fill in. I took it home, filled it in and sent it back. I was not feeling the best and was pessimistic not only about me but about the church, about the upheaval which was now a revolutionary war, and about the possibility of us doing anything about the miserable conditions in which so many people had to live. Dorothy looked at my responses to the questionnaire, weighed up what I said and sent back word that all things considered, did I know the stack in Queen's? The stack was the backside of the library, not the part where people milled around but the place where thousands upon thousands of books stood silently on their shelves. Nobody went in there except when looking for a book somebody had specially asked for or to do concentrated research. I knew it of course. So she said that according to my estimate of myself and my potential I should apply for a job there, see nothing but books for the rest of my working life and never have to set eyes on more than one human being at a time.

She said that with irony of course, but there was truth in it. At that time it seemed all I was fit for. However, she also suggested that Magee College was offering a Masters degree course in Community Education; why should I not go for it?

It was typical of Dorothy's perceptiveness and I was grateful for it. In Magee I was fortunate to meet Tom Lovett, one time bus driver, now a university lecturer and later founder of the Ulster People's College and Professor. We shared ideas about community education and development at a time when nobody seemed sure what community meant and many were doubtful about what education meant; there were so many competent people who loved learning but hated education.

Paolo Freire had opened up fresh ideas about how people could base their education on their own experience rather than on someone else's; Ivan Illich had published his radical ideas about deschooling society. Students were excited by the possibility of rethinking education from top to bottom – radically rethinking. During the following two years I studied along with a small group, including Sean Mc Mahon, who was quite properly offended when without malice I asked him how his travel guide was coming along. I should have known that Sean was an accomplished writer about people, history and places. Sammy Smyth was one of our group too, at that time public relations officer for the Ulster Defence Association, the loyalist military organisation. Tom Lovett was indignant about notions some people still had about education. Academics could say without blushing that working class people could not think in concepts; they could deal only with the here and now and concrete things, they could not plan for the future, preferring immediate satisfaction; they could not sustain attention for longer than a few minutes and so on. These ideas were widely accepted for a long time by people who should have known better. Sean O'Casey with a withering contempt for the class from which he had the honour to spring, inserted in 'The Shadow of a Gunman' a stage direction that 'like all of her class Minnie is not able to converse very long on the one subject'. He was one of many. But with all that there were other ideas around in the nineteen seventies which meant that for the first time the great potential of people for learning and teaching was being recognised, most importantly by people themselves. If we could bring local communities into contact with universities and universities with local communities, they would learn a lot from each other.

While I was at Magee a group of people went up to the College from West Belfast to hear Ivan Illich giving a talk about radical change in education. On the way home in the minibus there was an unusual silence. Then someone asked, 'Well, what did you think of Illich's ideas?' Pause. Then, 'Well, good, but didn't we find all that out in Ballymurphy long ago?'

Indeed so we did. In time the richness of learning among our neighbours would be recognised, and our ability to communicate our learning would be recognised also. There would always be snobs of course who would mock the idea that any learning was possible without them and their curricula. An official in the Belfast Education and Library Board, when told people were running classes in a front room in our Springhill housing estate where they decided what and whom they wanted to talk about and listen to, and paid expenses by handing round a secret bag like the Legion of Mary, swelled in indignation and said that was foolish. 'It's like bringing industry back to the houses as well.' As a matter of fact that seemed a good idea too but one thing at a time. She did not foresee the age of home computers.

I came home from Magee one day and was asked did I hear what happened to Sammy Smyth. He knew it might, he thought it would come from one of his own loyalist associates. He had refused a job in London saying he was not going to run away from it. He had been shot dead that afternoon as he opened his front door.

Studying is all very well but you have to survive. One possibility was to teach. We had classes in the Community House, now becoming known as 123 from the number on the door. Fees paid by the education authorities for teaching some of these adult classes were a help. Then the recently created Upper Springfield Resource Centre advertised for a Director and I got the job which lasted for just over three years, when I stepped aside and someone younger and fresher took my place. Some of us believed that in difficult times we got beyond our useful life in a job like that after three years. Frank Cahill, who was one of the most brilliant and least rewarded community workers in the district, was chairman of the Management Board.

Church officials did not ask me how I was going to survive, possibly assuming my family would take care of that. My family were always generous but they had their own lives and families to look after and they should not have to take on the responsibilities of church officials and myself. Church law provided for retired priests but church officials did not discuss this – since they would not even meet me – nor did any church official ask me what I needed. One friendly priest came in one day and handed me I think it was £20 which had a lot more value then than now. The rent of the house, about £5 a week, was stiff enough in those days.

When the news broke about my retirement and the row following it some Quaker friends came to the rescue. So did Brian Smeaton, the Church of Ireland priest who was working in the Shankill area at the time. He introduced us all to Richard Hauser, a sociologist living in London. Richard was Jewish; some of his people had escaped from the Nazi persecution, some did not escape. He spent his life studying and reporting on social conditions in various places and had done a report for the government in Dublin some years before this on conditions in homes for young offenders. He was one of the few who pleaded the cause of the Kurds while it was still public policy to hide what was happening to them. His wife Hepzibah was the sister of Yehudi Menuhin and an accomplished pianist. She could have had a brilliant musical career too but this was overshadowed by her attachment and devotion to Richard and his work. Richard Hauser offered us financial help and this was gratefully received, thus making up an ecumenical team of Presbyterians, Catholics, Anglicans, Jews and Quakers and the rest of us working together.

In 1975, when the disagreement and row between Bishop Philbin and myself became public, Ulster Television stopped communicating with me. The reaction of the editor of the Irish News, Terry O Keefe, to episcopal disfavour was different. In spite of the row about the review he had no difficulty about my writing anything about anything. Another friend before and after the 1975 disagreement was Moore

Wasson, who went on asking me to do broadcasts for the BBC. I said perhaps it might create difficulties for him and he replied that he wanted religious broadcasts and rows did not enter into it. J.G. McGarry, founder of The Furrow in Maynooth, said, 'Keep on writing'. So I went on doing things I had been doing before, writing here and there and broadcasting here and there as the occasion arose.

Many people, especially in the North, do not get credit for being as flexible and open as they really are. Falling out with a bishop and remaining trustee of The Furrow which is published in Maynooth should not have been possible if all the things people say about the church were true. There have always been people in the church who are confident enough in themselves to make their own decisions about whom they should work with and it is not easy to stop them doing it.

One of my priest friends said to me much later, when speaking about a particularly awkward clerical colleague, 'He's almost as awkward as you are'. It is not pleasant being looked on as awkward when you think you are just being normal. It was not nice during and after the 1975 row but friends made it almost all right. If we had all been able to talk out matters oftener and sooner in the church things would have been even better.

People should be free to talk and to find out what they want to know but they were not. At that time people often asked government for public inquiries, most often about misbehaviour of military and police. Such requests were mostly refused. So in 1978 we held the first public inquiry organised not by government but by local people about their own affairs and under their own authority. It was about education. We believed we should never have to depend on governments to hold public inquiries into things which concerned us. Some years later other public inquiries followed, organised by residents in different places.

The submissions people made to this inquiry in the Resource Centre we published word for word. If we just made a summary of them, it might be selective, or people might believe it was. Some said the submissions would be repetitive. They were not, and the views expressed at the Inquiry by parents, teachers, pupils, educationalists and others were striking examples of the wisdom and idealism of people who most of the time were never listened to. We published the verbatim Report with the help of money from the City Council, who were persuaded to give it by Councillor Paddy Devlin and colleagues. It was printed locally and bound in the print shop run by John McKeague in the east side of the city. Alex Reid and I had been talking to him often. We might as well give him the business. He did a good job which we could afford with the City Council's help. This was when politicians and governments and church officials were telling their public we could not live and work together and they would have to send in the soldiers to make us do it.

Years later John was shot dead in that shop amid accusations of very serious and very non-political wrongdoing.

When I went to his funeral, a reporter wanted to know was it not strange that a Catholic priest should attend the funeral of a well-known loyalist military activist. The answer was simple, Nobody is going to tell us who our friends are and what we should do about them. John did a lot of awful things but he was willing to talk to us, while others with more claims to charity and respectability refused.

The residents gave their Education Report to the British minister in charge of education at the time, Lord Peter Melchett. He was young and seemed to have ideas; people could talk to him, agree and disagree with him, and he assured us that he would make the education department look at it and pass their comments on to him. It was one of those rare moments of goodwill by a British minister. So the Department officials had to look at the Report which normally they would have ignored. We knew and he knew that as far as officials in the department were concerned that would be that; he admitted they were hard to budge.

When the Report was returned to him he sent their comments to us and we could see that the officials had defended themselves, making out that suggestions in the Report were either already tried, about to be tried, or tried and found wanting. It was what we expected, but at least we had got to the point where someone in government showed that our neighbours should not be ignored. So the public inquiry organised by people on their own behalf and on their own responsibility had been worth while. It was also a morale raiser which we very much needed and it gave us a new instrument to make us just little bit independent of governments.

In the following years there were not as many independent inquiries as we hoped but in time one public inquiry followed another, enough to show some independence. The important thing was that people had shown it is they and not the governments or churches or officials who should decide where and how we get information. In running public inquiries in the North the people were not always left to their own resources. There was a lot of help from our friends in the United States, Britain, Ireland and other countries. If people need information they must have it, and if they are refused it they have to find ways of getting it for themselves.

This idea was obscured when government tribunals were set up in Dublin which cost enormous amounts of money. These tended to reinforce the idea that public inquiries were so expensive and complicated that only governments could manage them. People in our local communities under pressure had shown this was not true. There are matters which are within the competence of government; others are well within the competence of whoever wants to deal with them. We wanted to be clear about which was which.

One way to understand what happened in the north of Ireland is to think of a constant creation of alternatives by people in crisis. They created alternative education, alternative welfare, alternative theatre, broadcasting, theological and political discussion, public inquiries and much else. They also created at various times alternative police and alternative armies. The authorities who had power over these in the past were and still are engaged in an equally constant struggle to regain total control of them. With only limited success, fortunately.

13

Peace without pacificism and pacificism without peace

When the Pope visited Ireland in 1979 we were in a sorry state in the North. The war was at its height and all attempts to persuade either church or state to talk to those waging it or even to those who could help to stop it were failing. There were mixed feelings about him coming. Some thought his visit would reawaken faith. Some thought it would help to ease the situation in the North. Others were less optimistic.

I was pessimistic. It was only four years after my retirement. I was still in an ecclesiastical wilderness, following the advice of family and friends to put on a cheerful face every time I appeared in public. Was trying to avoid crisis by raising temporary enthusiasm realistic?

Tim Pat Coogan asked me to 'write a speech you would like the Pope to make when he comes'. I said I would and tried not to let too much of the pessimism show. On the surface all was well and the church was still riding the crest of the wave as preparations were made for a million people to welcome him.

I thought what I wrote might not be published, with so much optimistic anticipation around, but it was. In the speech I had the pope saying, 'There are people who will kiss my hand today who will cheat on their spouses this evening'. He should ask us to assess where exactly we were and what we were doing and what we really believed and what he would do for us. But he probably would not. Bishop Eamon Casey, who later was publicly shamed, was one of the churchmen who led the celebratory singing that day. Father Michael Cleary whose reputation was tarnished after his death was another. And

Irish politicians prominent on the day were later understood to have been having affairs at the time. What else was going on? Who knew?

Soon after the article appeared I was in a bank and the manager asked me, 'How did you know?' Ireland is a small place but even with that I did not get it right, as future revelations were to show. Secret sex and secret money defeat even the most inquisitive of people.

The bank manager told me about what seemed at the time must be the Irish equivalent of Swiss bank accounts, but I was wrong here too because I misunderstood and probably he did too the scale of financial manoeuvring in and out of the country. He had been working in a border town, on the southern side, and sometimes unionist business people and farmers from the other side of the border would show interest in the Irish language, saying how intrigued they were by a second language being used so near at hand. They might ask what their own names would be in Irish. Some time later an account might open somewhere, on the southern side, in a name which was the Irish equivalent of Sammy's or Billy's or Nathaniel's.

I did not go to where the Pope was. I went to Donegal instead. His refusal to come to the North was a sad blow for people, many of whom nevertheless went to Drogheda or Knock or the Phoenix Park to visit him. Many republicans went and heard his vehement attack on those who were fighting the British government, with no reference to bad government. They knew his speeches were written for him by an Irish bishop and as he read them in a language foreign to him, he probably did not feel the full force of the words he was using. Although he was a demonstrative man, kissing the ground on arrival in a host country and making other significant gestures to underline his words, yet he used the phrase, 'I beg of you, on my knees I beg of you' to stop the war, and yet he remained standing. It would have been more according to his ways if he had suited action to words and knelt down. If so his words would have had an added drama. One might well wonder then whether this message was the most important one for him. His purpose was to attract the love and loyalty of the people rather than to alter the course of Irish politics. But we can only surmise. As far as the course of politics and the war were concerned, it did not signify. People had already discussed the moral problems of war and revolution and had solved them one way or another. Either it was morally acceptable to fight a bad government or it was not and the Pope's visit was not going to make much difference to combatants and their opponents who had already made up their minds and had had the past ten years and more in which to do so.

Republicans and nationalists who believed with all due respect to the churches that war against a bad government was legitimate attended the assemblies to see the Pope and listen to him. His visit provided a lull in the storm, but the storm became even fiercer afterwards.

We expected most unionists would keep a dignified silence during the visit, and hoped the rest would not use the opportunity to attack Catholic areas, many of whose residents were away from home.

Some time before the papal visit I got a phone call from two loyalist friends. They wanted to know if they could get a meeting with Cardinal Ó Fiaich. Yes, of course they could, Tomás Ó Fiaich was willing to be friends with everyone and meeting him was only a matter of finding spots in diaries.

Why did they want to meet him particularly? It is always convenient for people to know in advance what a conversation is to be about. They wanted to ask the Cardinal to use his influence to get the Pope to visit the North. After all, they said, all he has to do is cross the border and go along a narrow corridor to Armagh. They said not only would he be safe but he would be welcome and greeted with courtesy. None of us had any reason to disbelieve them. They met the Cardinal and he accepted their good faith.

We were surprised that the two loyalists wanted to ask Tomás to use his influence to get the Pope to come to the north of Ireland. Tomás assured them – and us – he would do what he could. But Tomás was no match – any more than any other Irish bishop – for the policies and practices of the Vatican. If the Pope came to the North in the context of a visit to the rest of Ireland this would be interpreted as a statement that Ireland is one, whereas if he came in the context of a visit to Britain this would be taken as a statement that the North is part of Britain. That diplomatic problem could have been solved if people had been asked about it, including Protestant people in the North. Requests for the Pope to come were refused, so when he came to Ireland and Britain he refused to visit the one place which could be said to need him most. It was a sad reminder that the comforting of one and a half million people of whom nearly half were Catholics had to take second place to the needs of Vatican diplomacy. Vatican policy was to support Britain and hopefully be supported by it in the European Community. In the Vatican's time-scale the Red Hand Commandos would pass away, so might Irish republicans and so certainly would Cardinal Ó Fiaich but the diplomatic links between Britain and the Vatican would be designed to go on forever. Those links were unproductive always and corrosive often, but the bureaucrats of the Vatican went on thinking in terms of the nineteenth century when the British might oppress Catholics at home but were able to provide good roads and protection for missionaries within the empire. One must not forget how useful the Roman empire had been in its day. And in these modern times the Vatican might well aspire to become the greatest spiritual influence in the European Union. And there was the hope that in the midst of all this the dream of reconverting England might be realised if not through popular friendship then through official cooperation. It was a poor bargain, but Vatican bureaucrats went for it. And we suffered for it.

Whether the Pope came to the North or not was a matter of diplomacy and politics, not of Protestant goodwill or Catholic need. In the coming years we were to have visits from President Clinton and the Dalai Lama, from Queen Elizabeth and Archbishop Desmond Tutu. But the Pope decided not to come. It was a curious situation where both Catholics and Protestants wanted him to come and he refused. We now realised once again how isolated we really were. We were among the few Catholics in the world who were in an ecclesiastical limbo. Our Catholic neighbours were disappointed.

Our Protestant friends were too, for one reason or another. One of them phoned me shortly before the papal visit and said, 'You know this visit by the Pope?' 'Yes'. 'Well, how would it be if I went to it?' 'You would be very welcome.' We talked about the three main venues for the visit. 'By the way, if you don't mind me asking, are you going just to watch or for a spiritual experience or because it is a big occasion you would like not to miss?' 'Well, as a matter of fact I'd like to bring along a hot dog stand.' There was something about the suggestion that made me uneasy but I could not see at once what it was. 'Billy', I said, 'that seems a good idea. But if you do, I'd advise you to go to Drogheda rather than Phoenix Park in Dublin. The Park is going to have enormous crowds, Knock is too far away but Drogheda would give you easy passage in and out. But there's something bothering me and I don't know what it is. Can I phone you back?'

A short while later I knew what it was and phoned him back. 'Billy, I still think Drogheda is the best place, but there's something you have to think about. I'm sure the people will be corralled into sections in the grounds and not be able to move about very much. That means you will not necessarily have a passing trade which is what you need'. 'True, I see that.' 'And also something you would not have thought of. I don't know what exactly is going to happen, but if there is a Mass there, a lot of people will go fasting. And there is nothing less conducive to the sale of hot dogs than a fasting population, no matter how big it is.' 'True.' 'And afterwards everybody will probably be dashing back home.' He gave up the idea of the hot dog stand. I do not know whether he ever went to see the Pope because I forgot to ask him.

In Belfast we needed work, we needed respect, we needed peace. Church officials talked peace but often encouraged war if waged by the right people. Peace was easy to talk about, pacifism was more difficult. Violence, peace and pacifism were seldom defined by our orators and experts. We had to find our own definitions. Father Dan Berrigan, Jesuit and total pacifist, visited us and gave a reading from his book The Catonsville Nine with members of our People's Theatre. This was in the early seventies in a little hall which did not survive the following turbulent years. On another occasion in Conway Mill he debated with Father Verbeek, a Catholic priest member of the Green Party in the European Parliament. Dan took the absolute pacifist position that attack in response to aggression was not acceptable, and even defending yourself by force was to be avoided. Father Verbeek argued that while it was a heroic ideal to give up one's life rather than use force against anyone, it had to be left to the people in any trouble spot to decide what they should do when confronted with evil. Their decision should be respected, whatever it was. A total pacifist could give up his or her own life, but what about those who had a duty to protect others – their families, their homes?

This was not just a theoretical question for our neighbours. They had to face and answer it every day. Most of us believed we had not only a right but a duty to defend ourselves and those for whom we were responsible. One evening we watched a film of people in Nicaragua, supporters of the revolution, saying the Rosary together.

This made us realise how we in Ireland had become shamefaced about opposition to bad government, even when our opposition to it was gentle. The film made a bold statement that revolutionaries could be deeply religious people. In Ireland this had been admitted but only about revolutionaries who eventually turned out to have been on the right side. As schoolchildren we were encouraged to believe Franco was on Christ's side and even to write poems in his honour when really he was a revolutionary against a lawfully elected government. Moral principles can be changed when powerful people demand it.

The churches gave us little help and the government none at all as we faced the moral question: when your home and person are attacked, when your neighbours are under fire, does our religion really require us to be total pacifists? If people had believed that, there would not have been a Catholic home still standing in Belfast by the end of 1969.Two of our priests were shot dead by British soldiers in St John's Parish during the worst period of attacks. I was away on holidays on both occasions and sometimes felt a vague guilt about that, but there is no use worrying that you were not there when a tragedy happened. One of the priests had been a pharmacist, the other had been in the Merchant Navy and both had decided to turn aside from their professions and become priests.

If the two murdered priests, Noel Fitzpatrick and Hugh Mullan, had remained a pharmacist and a seaman, both of them might still be alive now. So what does God have in mind if He inspires people to take on one way of life rather than another? Does He mean that ten years as a priest will serve His interests better than forty years as a merchant seaman or a pharmacist?

Hugh had radical ideas about what the church should do, particularly to relieve the poverty around us. Noel was more contemplative and content to bring people into the church, to preach and give the sacraments, visit and be the model of the ideal traditional priest. Hugh was shot dead in 1971 when internment without trial was brought in and Noel about a year later when an onslaught was made on people in Springhill housing estate, one of a series of military onslaughts of which Bloody Sunday in Derry was the most severe and notorious.

Few people want to talk about those onslaughts even many years afterwards. In a local public inquiry into the attacks in which Hugh Mullan was murdered as he tried to attend a wounded man, one witness who told what he saw and experienced was telling the story in public for the first time, more than a quarter of a century after the event. People who lived through those disasters in Belfast, Derry and so many other places suffered hurts which governments and churches did not recognise, and which people themselves did not want to talk about any more than previous generations wanted to talk to us about what happened to them in the nineteen twenties. Most of what I learned about Belfast in the twenties I did not learn from my parents but pieced together one way or another as the years went by.

One set of killings my parents did talk about because it seared the souls of our people as nothing else did was the murder of the McMahon family by the policeman Nixon and his gang. That was in 1922 and apart from that we heard little of the details and of what life was really like and how people like my father would be stowed away under the stairs when people knew the murder gangs were out. The murder gangs came out from the RUC barracks in Brown Square and Springfield Road.

If Hugh and Noel had been murdered in El Salvador or Colombia or under a communist regime, much more would have been said publicly about it, but this was Ireland, the British government was in control and the church leaders had a softly-softly approach to them, whether through promises or fear or both. Nearly thirty years later when local people held their public inquiry into the deaths of Hugh Mullan, Noel Fitzpatrick and our other neighbours, they had to get over their severe trauma to do it. It was a matter of pride that they did. It was a shame they had to.

Radio and television people liked to ask, 'Are you a pacifist?' My answer always was, 'Yes, I am'. Then they would demand that I condemn the IRA or whatever military group was of interest to them. When I refused they would say this is a strange kind of pacifist who will not condemn those who are waging a revolutionary war, attacking police, military, people and shops. The practical answer was that a pacifist will do whatever is possible to prevent a war happening, will try to lessen its impact while it is going on, will try to stop it. And that is that.

We needed a philosophy, or a theology of pacifism but we did not have one. The churches were not pacifist in any sense and showed no sign of becoming so. They wanted an end to armed conflict, which is not the same as being pacifist, creating or sustaining peace.

Condemning one party or another in our conflict just stifled discussion and made a bad situation worse. It had nothing to do with pacifism; it had everything to do with defeating one side or another and it was an intellectually lazy way to assert one's own respectability while changing nothing. If you condemned those whom the government condemned your words could be broadcast perhaps on the BBC's World Service; if you criticised government, your words most of the time might not be broadcast even in your own city. The definition of right and wrong was in the hands of those who could broadcast furthest. So however much clergy and commentators might throw up their hands in horror, we had to create a reasoned definition of pacifism which would satisfy our needs not just those of an oppressive government or of people seeking undemanding respectability. Condemning people made us look respectable but did not stop the war.

We had had our lessons. Hundreds of pacifist and peace groups had sprung up in Europe between the two world wars, all saying that war should never be allowed to happen again. Generous, courageous people created one initiative after another between France, Germany and other European countries, healing anger and dissolving the hatred which had been artificially and ruthlessly created to enable the First World War to be waged. Franz Stock, a German priest was one of them. But he saw the collapse of peace movements at the outbreak of war and had to spend the war years ministering to French prisoners of war and attending the executions of many of them.

Pacifist groups flourished between the wars, trades unions declared themselves pacifist and churches came out against war in all circumstances. However, when the war started, the pacifists, including some members of the Society of Friends, were beaten outside Belfast City Hall by citizens who were furious that they were still pacifist, while the trades unions entered vigorously into the war effort and remained there as the war became more vicious, then total. So did the churches. With all that in mind and remembering James Connolly who believed the First World War in Europe could be stopped by an uprising of poor people starting in Ireland, and was executed for it, some of us were sceptical about the usefulness of the peace groups created in Ireland during the 30 years from 1970 on.

A Church of Ireland priest and myself, visiting a peace group in Athlone, were surprised to find it was run by the local military and their spouses. They asked us not to refer to what was happening in the North as a war because, they said, that made it respectable. War as respectable did not seem a pacifist idea or even a peaceful one. Attending a meeting of a peace group later in Belfast I learned that the proposal for the meeting came not from the peace group but from the military whose representative was there and said he would report back to his superior officers what was said at the meeting. The distrust of local communities was such that no other community representatives who had been invited turned up. Needless to say we did not say much to each other at that meeting. You become careful of those who cry 'Peace'. You need to know if they really mean it.

Dan Berrigan, his brother Philip who died in 2003 and others like them courageously took on the military in the United States of America and went to jail for it. But while we respected Dan's ideals and way of life, in our own situation we could not accept the absolute pacifism he proposed

Although no church engaged in real discussion about peace and pacifism, Catholic clergy were instructed to speak against the military republicans and their campaign. I became more and more puzzled by what bishops asked us to say from our pulpits condemning the IRA. The Catholic church has clear rules about war and revolution. It would be surprising if after nearly 2000 years of trying to solve human problems it did not have clear rules about them. It had had to think things out and arrive at realistic compromises between what was ideal and what we can achieve. Did Catholic teaching then really justify these condemnations from our pulpits in the name of Catholic morality? You might have strong reasons for saying a war should not start or should stop but were we right in saying Catholic moral law demanded that the IRA should stop fighting? We cannot afford to demand too much of people in the name of Catholic morality because if we do, Catholic morality will fall into disrepute. We have to be honest about its limitations.

So in 1974, after we had read one of these condemnatory statements in our churches against armed revolution, I visited a priest whom I greatly respected, a man whose intellectual ability and integrity would have fitted him for any position in the church but whose health was never up to it, perhaps fortunately for his peace of mind. I met him and another priest in his parochial house.

I asked: 'People may want to say the IRA is doing wrong, but can we say that Catholic moral teaching strictly speaking demands it?' The answer came more firmly than I expected: 'There are seven conditions which have to be fulfilled before a Catholic can take part in a revolution with a clear conscience – and all but one have been fulfilled in this situation'. The missing one, he believed, was that the IRA did not have a reasonable chance of success and therefore its campaign could make a bad situation worse. The other conditions were fulfilled.

'But', I said, 'that is not what we preached last Sunday. What we read out was a condemnation without exceptions or explanations.' No, he replied, but what we read out is the official policy and teaching of the local Church here as decided by the bishop. I turned to the other priest. He agreed.

I did not argue. I had too much respect for them both to get into a difficult and delicate discussion where we would have to disagree. I went to another priest in another part of the city and put the same question to him. He said, 'I have no moral problem with the armed campaign of the IRA as far as strict interpretation of Catholic moral teaching is concerned'. In other words, if you want to oppose the military campaign, you have to find other reasons for doing so. But that is not what we preached last Sunday. 'We have to pass on the official church teaching as given by the bishop, no matter what our personal views are.'

I left it at that. But I did not want to preach what I did not believe and I did not believe that Catholic moral teaching forbade people to fight against a bad government which would not be reformed. You may find strong reasons why people should not fight a bad government and the cruel and powerful revenge governments take on a whole people is one of them, but you have to be careful not to destroy confidence in moral teaching by pretending it demands more than it really does. It is not the people's fault if fighting is their last resort in defence of their own life and dignity. Governments have vast resources to make peace if they want to, the people do not. The first duty to make sacrifices for peace is on government, not on the people governed. But governments often undermine their own credibility and the people's faith in them by what they do. They equip themselves more earnestly to stifle dissent than to change bad government into good.

But fortunately there were people among us prepared to go searching for peace. Political conversations were going on all through these years although the propaganda persisted that our people could not talk to each other.

Eric Gallagher at some time President of the Methodist church asked for a meeting between himself, a colleague and members of the republican movement who could talk authoritatively about the aims of the movement, including the military campaign. This meeting was set up, inappropriately, in the Imperial Hotel in Dundalk. Seán Mac Stiofáin was there with Joe Cahill. For Fr Alec Reid, a member of the Redemptorist Order famed for his peace making, and myself the job was to stay quiet while the others talked. They did, or rather, Seán did while Joe, who looked upon himself more a doer than a talker, listened and said little. Some of the time he was listening to the news on the radio and from time to time so were we all.

Before the discussion began I went down to the hotel lobby, leaving Seán and Eric talking. In the car going home after the meeting Eric was a bit quiet. He had been surprised at that conversation with Seán while I was in the lobby. Part of it was about the difference between modern and classical Greek. Eric, like many of his colleagues, had believed what their parties and churches were saying about the republicans, that you could not talk to them; they were simply vandals, without any political programme or culture. The propaganda was repeated so often that the propagandists came near to believing it themselves. A discussion about the differences between modern and classical Greek was not what was expected. Nor a rational discussion about democratic politics. But when they met republicans, this is what they got. The reason governments kept republicans from broadcasting and discussion in public was not that they might sometimes talk violence – it could be edited out if they did – but because they would so often talk sense. The republicans did not worry too much about that hostile propaganda; they had come through worse traumas than that. Occasionally however their irritation showed. Two prominent republicans were driving with us to a meeting with some unionists. At the time a few Irish politicians were behaving badly on visits abroad, drank too much or were indiscreet with nice women. What they did in private was of no interest to us but in public they were representing us and our neighbours. Even while some of us were visiting the United States to speak about what was happening in Ireland these people were undermining the dignity of Irish people by their behaviour. And they were going at public expense while others were relying on the hospitality of our American friends. In the car that evening on our way to the meeting I must have said something about this. One of our republican friends said, 'Yes, they do sometimes misbehave and that should not happen', or words to that effect, a very mild criticism. It was ironic that here were two republicans, both total abstainers, both following a code of personal behaviour so strict that in later times it seemed too much even for strong republicans, lamenting the behaviour of politicians who were generally considered so respectable.

Our talks with loyalists were always interesting but seldom secret. We kept our word about confidentiality as to what was said at meetings, but what we talked about was not necessarily unknown to police. One time, in the late seventies we had a meeting in Dundalk, a meeting shrouded in such secrecy that we were sure nobody knew or had seen us coming or going. But John McKeague of the Red Hand Commando who had been at the meeting was able to phone up next day and say the peelers knew what we had for our tea. I suspected they knew because John had told them. So at meetings one talked only in general terms to make sure nothing was said to help anybody to finger anyone else.

On the train to Dublin one day going along the corridor to get a cup of coffee I met two Professors, John Barclay of the Presbyterian College and Cornelius O'Leary of Queen's, a Catholic. I asked them why all the church leaders did not come together and tell Paisley publicly his day was over and he must stop abusing people. John said, 'If Presbyterian clergy said that out loud, half their congregations would walk away from them.'

I never approached religious friends again to ask them to unite about anything. I could see no point in it if people were so afraid of Jesus Christ's solution to such problems. When his followers talked about leaving him he was willing to let them go. God is used to small numbers.

John was nearly right about half the congregations walking away if the Presbyterians united with others against the agitator; about 43 per ceny of the votes of Protestants went to Paisley. If 43 per cent of congregations walked away that was serious not only for the clergy but for their wives and families. In theory the celibacy of Catholic clergy means they do not have to worry about that and so can afford to be more daring. It works sometimes, not always. For them the fear of demotion and loss of official favour can be as real as worry about home and family. Some Protestant clergy who showed courage for change did lose their congregations or had to leave the country, or found it difficult to get a congregation to accept them. Church officials could have been more sensitive to the reality of how clergy had to live and been more willing to support them when they got into trouble. The Drumcree saga and much else showed how fearful church officials were in spite of all the promises of wisdom and strength they said the Lord had made to them.

On the wall of his study John Barclay's poster-size list of the men forced out of their ministry or out of the country wryly showed their 'crimes': this one had prayed with Roman Catholics, that one had ecumenical tendencies, this one had shown Romanist tendencies, that one had done something else, all innocent but in Ireland's northeast serious matters, not only for comfort but for survival. A list made possible by northern policy which created the situation and by southern power struggles which helped to perpetuate it.

You could not blame John or his Presbyterian colleagues who were so vulnerable and unprotected. The blame lay with leaders who refused to join together to say 'No' to Christian bullies, or worse, became Christian bullies themselves. Some of us thought that the fear of each other could be lessened if we all insisted on open discussion and independence. But fear ruled everywhere.

14

The McBride Principles

I was invited to Glasgow in the late seventies to talk to people there about our situation in the north of Ireland. The Catholic archbishop there was cross about it.

The only other time I had been to Glasgow was in the nineteen sixties to talk to a Catholic clergy conference about ecumenism. That was a two-day conference and I wondered why we could not get all the business done in one day. I found out why. The first day's proceedings were dull enough, although it was interesting to hear priests talking about life in Glasgow where they suffered the same artificially induced sectarianism as we did.

When the day's talking and listening were over some of the clergy met in the local parochial house and for the first time in my life I saw punch being prepared. The chat beforehand, the expectation, the carrying in of the steaming bowl, the reverential mixing of whatever was to mix with the whiskey – I sat there sticking out like a sore thumb, being the only one present who did not drink whiskey. They were very kind and got me something else. In Maynooth most of the students decided not to touch the stuff because whiskey was the downfall of some good people, including a few clergy. There is an aura of sweet destructiveness about whiskey which seems not to hang around vodka or beer or even gin. The very word seems to spell trouble.

The drinking of the punch in that Scottish presbytery was ceremonial. I saw the sheer joy of conviviality. It was like the first time I saw two French people in a Paris cafe enjoying food in a way we never seemed to do at home, the looking – the tasting, the eating, the faces reflecting the pleasure, even the wiping up with a hunk of

New medical centre

Dr. J. F. McKenna (left), chief medical officer, pictured with Dr. Mary Keane, Dr. Kevin Wilson, Dr. Michael Cullen, Dr. Mary Cashell and Dr. Daniel Delargy, after he had officially opened their new Medical Centre at North Parade, Ormeau Road, Belfast.

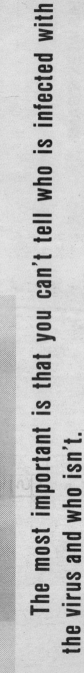

The most important is that you can't tell who is infected with the virus and who isn't.

One faithful partner is best. If you're in any doubt, use a condom. Finally, don't inject drugs, or at least never share equipment.

OF IGNORANCE.

5777. ISSUED BY THE UNITED KINGDOM HEALTH DEPARTMENT

bread afterwards, for which we would have been driven out of polite society at home.

When the punch began to flow in the clerical gathering the talk began to flow as well. And one of the priests whispered to me, 'Now you know why the conference is for two days and not just one'. Nobody got tight, everybody talked and the second day of the conference was a vast improvement on the first. I was sorry to have to leave for an afternoon plane home.

My second visit to Glasgow was overshadowed by the ghost of exclusion. In Ireland things had changed for the worse; tragedies had happened and more were to come. The group who asked me over this time had hired a hall belonging to a religious community. Some days before the meeting they got word from Dr Winning, the archbishop, that the meeting was not to take place or if it was, it had to take place somewhere other than in church premises. The group were outraged and told everybody, including Winning, that the meeting would go ahead wherever the group decided it should. And so it did. Later I heard that Winning said he did not want troublemakers coming around.

I wrote to tell him he must never make judgments about me without doing me the courtesy of talking to me. I got no reply and I hoped the forecasts that he could become pope would prove unfounded. They did of course.

Some years later I was invited to another meeting in Glasgow which also had to do with the political situation in Ireland. At the last moment before the meeting we were refused entry to the hotel which had accepted the booking. We had to go out to the local public park where fortunately the weather was not too cold to have our meeting there. One of the speakers was Ken Livingstone whose irritation was tempered by his experience of being excluded so often already.

Our churches were forever praising Jesus for knocking around with all sorts, the unpopular tax people, the frightening military people, the despised prostitute people, the arrogantly nicknamed 'lower classes', people up trees and coming down from rooftops, but they seemed to think he really wanted his followers to exclude people and just never let on about it at the time. If Jesus had wanted a religion of exclusion, though, he would have said so and he didn't. Many Christians believed they could be safe only if they excluded others from sight and sound. One of the principles on which the Northern Ireland state was founded was that of exclusion of Catholics and some others from influence in public life.

One of the most successful answers to anti-Catholic exclusion and viciousness in employment was the McBride Principles campaign. The Principles were a set of conditions which employers were asked to honour before investing in any enterprise involving Northern Ireland. Oliver Kearney, the most gifted and best informed person on this complicated problem, spearheaded a campaign in Ireland, the United States and other countries.

The campaigners asked American and other foreign companies to place industry in the north of Ireland only if they accepted and fulfilled a programme of fair employment and that no American investment should occur unless with the same conditions. The states and city councils were asked to cooperate on the grounds of humanity and fairness but also because as long as discrimination continued there could be no democratic settlement in Ireland's northeast. Many American states and city councils accepted the Principles. Patrick Doherty was working in the office of the powerful financial Comptroller of New York City. He worked quietly and effectively for years, first to help create the campaign and then keep it alive and working. Alan Hevesi, who was New York City financial Comptroller when the campaign started, gave Patrick freedom to see to it. The campaign caught the imagination of Irish Americans and others. Naturally there was opposition to the campaign as an increasing number of states and city councils adopted the Principles. The British government had needed discrimination to keep control in Ireland, although it should have been clear for a long time that cooperation rather than cruelty could have strengthened their hold on it. Governments learn slowly if at all and the McBride Principles campaign, depending on the goodwill, hard work and hard-earned dollars of Irish Americans, won in the end; the British government spent and lost many millions of dollars on its failure to destroy it. As the states and city councils continued to accept the Principles and as they were supported by those in America who controlled vast sums of money hardly imaginable by us, the British government became increasingly frustrated.

When Patrick Doherty was putting together a panel of sponsors for the Principles he phoned and discussed some names. Sean McBride was willing to be the principal sponsor. The surgeon John Robb, who was proud of the Presbyterian liberal tradition to which he belonged, was suggested, and Inez McCormack, a trade unionist who always opposed cruelty in employment and supported the dignity of workers. Father Brian Brady was the fourth sponsor, a long-time human rights campaigner. In a reasonable society the Principles would scarcely have raised an eyebrow but in the northeast of Ireland they were greeted as if the proposers of them were subversives. The credit due to John and Inez, Brian and Sean could not be over-stated. Nor could the work of Oliver Kearney, whose expert knowledge of the realities of anti-Catholic discrimination could not be matched by opponents of the Principles although they had immense resources to attempt it.

Some of the opposition to the Principles surprised us, especially from Irish Catholics flown over at British government expense to persuade Americans not to adopt them.

Leaders of the Irish churches went to the United States to argue against the Principles. Some church officials in Ireland had encouraged or condoned unfair employment in Ireland for much the same reasons that others encouraged or condoned it in South Africa until the internal dynamic of that situation persuaded them to change their strategy. Some Catholic trade unionists went over too. One of them had already told us some years before when we asked him for help to create jobs in our district, 'The business of the trades unions is to protect the jobs that are there, not to create new ones'. Catholic members of the Alliance Party went also. We could not know how much all this first class travel and accommodation cost the London and Dublin governments in their fight against the Principles of fair employment. Nor could we estimate the costs met by those Americans and others who out of their own pockets offered the hospitality of their homes to people from Ireland coming to plead for fairness in Ireland through the Principles.

Some of the Irish people representing the British government showed naiveté. They seemed to think, some Irish politicians did too, that in America they were so far away from their home base that they could say anything that would help their case. A trade unionist proclaimed himself a representative not only of workers but of Irish Catholics.

As politicians and city councillors discussed whether to adopt the Principles or not, it was startling to hear a Catholic member of the

Alliance Party lecturing American councillors on how they should study Northern Ireland as an example to Americans of how to govern a divided society! Such naiveté was embarrassing but it made our efforts less difficult, especially when the chairman of the hearing belonged to the African-American community who was well aware of how industrial cruelty worked and just as aware of the unfair arguments so often used to defend it. He had heard them often enough and the arguments justifying a bad system were similar on both sides of the Atlantic.

I was at home when we got an urgent message from a McBride Principles hearing in America. A Catholic solicitor acting in the British interest was claiming to represent the Dublin government as well. Someone left the council chamber, went to a fax machine and sent word to us at Springhill. The team in Springhill sent a query about this to Dublin; the message came back that this man was doing nothing of the kind and had no authority to say he was. The man suffered the discomfort of being presented with Dublin's denial before he had even finished making his submission to the hearing and within minutes of having even started it.

It was discouraging at times to see who was opposing the Principles. A Northern Ireland civil servant was ordained into the Presbyterian church ministry, went to America, addressed many meetings there, sometimes accompanied by a Catholic priest, and used these opportunities to speak in favour of a flawed British system and against the kind of employment protection we were urging, now with more and more American and other international support. Most of the time those who went to the United States to oppose the Principles did not talk to the proposers or sponsors of them beforehand. They took their brief from British government departments. So apart from casual meetings in American council chambers, the Irish proponents and opponents did not have useful discussions about the Principles.

One of the arguments used by opponents was that they would discourage investors from investing in the north of Ireland. Our argument was that on the contrary, if the Principles of fair employment were accepted, we could promise them efficient workers who for the first time in our history we could guarantee were appointed not through lodge membership but through their ability to do the job. An Irish Catholic priest who later became a bishop told the Americans that the McBride Principles were wrong because they would not put one loaf of bread on the table. But they were not meant to; they were meant to ensure that fair employment would help put as many loaves on as many tables as possible in a peaceful society. But then he also told Americans there was a city parade in Belfast every St Patrick's Day just as there was elsewhere, a parade nobody had actually seen!

Arguments of different kinds, some good, some incompetent, were used against the Principles but when more and more cities and states accepted them, the opposition changed into a plea not to abandon the principles but to have them modified, for instance to exclude the name of Sean McBride and get another sponsor in his place. Among those who went to America with that message were some senior Catholic and Protestant churchmen. The SDLP then said it was opposed not to the Principles, which were fine, but to the campaign which put them forward. This was a small and useful step away from total opposition.

As the McBride Principles campaign went from east to west in face of expensive British opposition, gathering momentum from so many Americans, Irish-Americans and others, the effect began to be seen at home. In the end the British government had to introduce new fair employment legislation and the McBride Principles campaign can claim credit for pushing them towards it. At every stage of its progress into law this fair employment legislation was flawed. But once a government admits the principle of fair employment there is no going back however long it may take to produce real equality and real dignity with adequate laws to uphold them.

At some period during the nineteen eighties, because of the hospitality and dedication of friends in the United States and Canada, I was going over there about once every five months, sometimes for court cases, sometimes to talk about the situation at home, and about the McBride Principles if in an area where the Principles were being proposed and opposed.

15

From Ballymurphy to Boston

In the nineteen seventies we got a minibus. People in West Belfast like to travel but the situation at that time made it difficult, even dangerous. A Queen's University lecturer once said that people in West Belfast are 'solipsistic'. She meant inward-looking and maybe her remark increased the vocabulary of the university by a word, but we have a tradition of travelling, from the early Irish adventurers and traders to the modern pilgrims, work and holiday seekers. We travel to visit friends or because a political regime has refused us work or living space or just because we think travelling is a good thing.

One of our neighbours whose poetry and stories for her children helped to inspire the adult education programme of the Community House was asked if she would like to join a group of us going to Rome. Being used to the kind of local trips we usually made she said 'yes'. But she was also a little hard of hearing and when we told her she should see to her passport she revealed that she thought we had said we were going to Tyrone. She went along anyway, Rome and Tyrone being both worth a visit.

I thought, naively as it turned out, that it would be a good idea while in Rome to go and meet the Irish ambassador to the Vatican. At that time, the seventies, we were talking to everybody who would listen to us and we needed help. We wanted people in influential positions to understand what was happening to us. We wanted to sweep protocol aside and talk to whomever we wished to talk to. We had the right to do that. The Vatican had done nothing to help us as far as any of us could see. If the Vatican was informed about what was happening to members of the church in Ireland, would it be so indifferent?

So I went to see the Irish ambassador in the Vatican.

The rest of the party went to visit a countess to whom they were introduced by Lelia Doolan who was always one for thinking of colourful and interesting things to do. So they had the pleasure of having tea on the roof garden of a Roman house while I was less fortunate. The ambassador either knew nothing or pretended to know nothing. He seemed unable to grasp what I was saying about the real needs of our people at home. At the end of the interview I was escorted through the garden by one of his aides who said apologetically I should not judge the man too harshly. I thought very harshly of him. I wondered if some of our representatives abroad were letting us down through inefficiency and indifference. I learned later they were letting us down through government policy as well.

Looking back on it now I wonder at how we bothered to make approaches like these. Ambassadors are not going to take notice of people like us – a busload of people from Ballymurphy. It shows how desperate we were. Institutions heed other institutions, not people. And what government and churches see as the needs of diplomacy will always take first place over what people see as their needs. An English priest at that time remarked to us that the way to get a bishop in his country to do anything was to ask him, get his refusal, then phone him later to say, 'About that suggestion you made to me the other day, I thought it was rather good. Could you tell me again?' If he believed the idea was his own you were winning. It worked sometimes, he said, and was worth trying always.

But even when real persons in one institution speak with real persons in another institution, they have a pecking or listening or talking or heeding order.

In the very early seventies our neighbours talked to British army officers believing, wrongly, they could persuade them to have some respect for the people and their dignity. Meetings were held between residents, priests, bishops, army officers, community workers. Always the top brass on one side spoke to the top brass on the other. A major would speak to a senior curate, but if there was a bishop present he would speak to him, assuming the bishop was leader of his pack, or the senior curate, just as captain or major was leader of his. We sometimes tried to break through the conventions and have people of all kinds recognised as having the right to speak to people of all kinds. Most of the time we need not have bothered. Whatever conventions were broken in times of crisis, and times of crisis were the best times to break them, they would be set up again as soon as possible once the crisis was over.

The Vatican ambassador told me that every time anything important happened in the north of Ireland the first person round to the Vatican Secretary of State was whatever British representative was available. Due to the sectarian needs of the British state they considered it inadvisable until recent years to have a full ambassador at the Vatican. When international pressure came on Britain to improve its behaviour in Ireland following the failure of its final solution in 1969, it was considered necessary to upgrade British diplomatic presence in the Vatican.

In the diplomatic rush round to the Vatican's Secretary of State the British representative always got there first, perhaps because the Irish one was too old or unconcerned to make a race of it, or, as we later came to believe, because he was under instructions from Dublin not to hurry himself.

Some time after the Rome visit Monsignor Bruce Kent said I ought to speak to Archbishop Bruno Heim, to tell him directly what Catholics in our neighbourhood were going through. Heim, living on the edge of Wimbledon Common, was the Vatican representative in London. Bruce arranged the visit for me but there was not much benefit from that meeting either. For people in high places the issues are not the important thing; it is the person raising them. Trivialities spoken by a bishop or a lord will be given more weight than important concerns raised by a junior priest talking for his neighbours. The solution for that is not to put the people in high places off their perches but rather to make them irrelevant. The present hierarchical and class systems in church and state require us so-called ordinary people to let others speak for us to God, to ambassadors and even to judges in courts when we are demanding our rights. We have to be spoken for, which is unnecessary and degrading. I got talking to these people because there was a crisis but since they did not need to heed me we were back where we started. If the churches open their doors and minds they have a right to talk about every member being inspired by the Holy Spirit, not otherwise. And diplomats abroad should be made to render an account of their stewardship to the people who pay their salaries.

Faced with the powerlessness of people and the dependency of the Vatican on political and economic interests, we have either to dismantle the Vatican apparatus or make it irrelevant, otherwise the

Catholic church will not be of much help in ensuring the dignity of our people. People say you can be heard if you get into a high position but in order to get into a high position you may have to abandon most of what you wanted to get into a high position to achieve. And when you get into one high position, you will want to get to the next highest to be more effective, or more influential. The appetite grows by what it feeds on, as Shakespeare put it. Social and religious change will have to be made outside the ambit and structures of churches as they are at present. The impetus for change has always come from outside political parties rather than from inside them, and we can think the same way about churches.

Archbishop Heim was pleasant and courteous. But he was also in the same straitjacket as the Pope would be when visiting Ireland in 1979. The Pope's representative to the Irish people was not Heim but the Papal Nuncio in Dublin whose sphere of influence in theory was all Ireland. Heim was accredited to the London government but was not to concern himself with church affairs in the north of Ireland. The curious situation arose then that for political reasons Heim could not intrude into church affairs of the North because this would seem to say the North was part of Britain, while at the same time the Irish bishops had made it clear to the Papal Nuncio in Dublin that he should not go further north than Dundalk. So we in the north of Ireland were among the few Catholics in the world with no papal representative at all. And we were the people whom the Pope avoided in our time of trouble. We used to say jokingly that a time would come when Catholics as well as Protestants would be saying 'No Pope Here'. As far as papal presence in the North was concerned, there was no pope there anyway.

Archbishop Heim seemed interested, but when he asked what the church could do – he should have been told long before this – I was surprised that he seemed not to be aware of Cahal Daly whom at that time many of us looked on as one of the few senior churchmen who could bring intelligence and principle into our situation. It might help if Cahal were in touch with Heim. He might listen to him.

When Cahal was eventually appointed bishop of Down and Connor in 1983 the Papal Nuncio in Ireland, Monsignor Alibrandi, made one of his infrequent visits to the North for his installation. After the ceremony he remarked to a group of priests, 'Well, you got what you wanted, didn't you?'

Sometimes we thought we were making an impression telling high churchmen abroad the realities of our situation but most of the time it was frustrating. Concerned friends in the United States or England or elsewhere would direct us to a bishop who seemed open to persuasion. While talking to him you had to be careful not to alienate him by being critical of fellow bishops; it was like talking to politicians and making sure not to criticise their party leader. You had to take account also of the conservative views of most bishops and many Catholics. You had to realise that government propaganda from London and Dublin made all of us who protested against government policy into subversives. Once when talking to a bishop in America who was reckoned to be liberal I was desperate enough to try to pull aside the silk curtain between us and church reality.

'Bishop, do you know of any place in the world where practising faithful Catholics walk out of their homes on voting day, walk to the polling station and vote that their government should be disciplined by the vote if possible and by force of arms if necessary?' He was startled and that was good. 'Because that is what the recent vote in the north of Ireland means.' At that time Catholics had rejected the church leaders' demands not to vote for Sinn Féin which publicly recognised the right of people to fight against bad government as a last resort. The pro-republican vote was increasing. Although the Catholic church's moral code also recognised this right – the republicans were more theologically correct than the bishops – Irish churchmen would not admit such resistance could be morally lawful against a British government in Ireland. We were never given satisfactory reasons why it had been moral to fight against a lawful government in Spain in the thirties and immoral to fight against an unlawful one in Ireland any time.

The American bishop soon recovered his composure but since he was unwilling to discuss how bad a government had to be to provoke such a reaction from Catholics, there was little more to be said except polite farewells.

But we had friends abroad too, more and more as time went on. The first invitation I got to go to the United States to talk to people there showed how wrong I had been about America and Americans. It was in 1983 and we had been so taken in by the 'Four Horsemen', Kennedy, Carey, O'Neill and Moynihan, that it took a long time for us to realise that they gained more from us than we did from them. Dan

Berrigan said I should go to America and then an invitation came from a church group in Islip, New Jersey. I told them I preferred not to go even to explain what was happening in Ireland because we had been so disappointed by the churches at home. I tried to say as courteously as I could that churches had nothing to offer in solving human problems or realising human potential. They had something to do in our society but it was not that.

The group insisted, however, that they knew what oppressiveness meant, knew that churches were often disappointing but they still invited me to come.

I went and was grateful for it. I was introduced to a vibrant, generous and committed group of people who understood the connection between what was happening in Ireland and what was happening in oppressive situations in other countries. It was a much needed lesson that in the United States, Canada, Britain, Australia and so many other countries there are people who do not just talk about justice but are prepared to work and sometimes suffer for it. I had naively accepted too much of the British version of what Americans were like and of the Irish trust in the 'Four Horsemen' and was now getting rid of both.

Brendan Walsh, Willa Bickham and their family and friends in Baltimore, the Berrigans and their friends, the Logues in New Jersey, many friends whom I was to meet in the years that followed, people who used their resources great or small to help others in campaigns for justice and peace, these people made sense of our concept of a universal family of people who really believed what they said.

In the years after that Islip invitation I went over often. The hospitality of the good people there was wonderful but these visits were often filled with anxiety. Sometimes it was to attend court hearings where people were facing deportation or extradition, sometimes to talk to people about our situation in Ireland which often seemed to be going from bad to worse. I knew well that in talking at meetings or broadcasting I might undo years of patient work with one careless statement. We all had to take into account the sensitivities and ideals of people, their views on race and religion and how much or little they knew of the Irish situation already. Only the organisers of meetings could say how much or how little an audience was likely to know but people came to public meetings with so many different views and the organisers might never have seen most of them before. One could only go over to America or any other country with a long list of things worth saying and make a selection of them at short notice. We had not only to give information but to try to counter some of the vast amount of propaganda put out by the governments in London and Dublin aided by most of the media in the United States who relied on British Information Services to an alarming extent, as Catholic universities and publications did too.

The International Fund for Ireland was created after the Anglo-Irish Agreement in 1975 to help bring development to the north of Ireland without significant political change. When it was set up we were promised that this time there would be no discrimination, all would be treated fairly. As usual people in our area accepted the promises in good faith. After all, American money was involved and surely once you removed money from British government control it was at least a little more likely to be available for Catholics as well as others. But the IFI money was not allowed to get out of British control and the result was an immense and scandalous abuse in which rich people in the North got more money than they needed and poor people got next to nothing.

That was the hurt in that operation. The insult was when we went to the International Fund asking for capital for development, much less capital than was given to wealthy hotel owners who were well able to find capital in the ordinary way. We approached everybody we could think of with all the plans and guarantees we could possibly need. The chairman of the International Fund told us, 'The IFI was not set up to give out money for charity'.

We did not expect him to appreciate what an insult to our people that was. We saw unfolding the scandal of the waste of American money in Ireland, the waste of British money, the waste of Irish money, the waste of the talent of our neighbours. The anger we felt was deep and lasting. So we campaigned in Britain, Ireland and America to try to have the International Fund used properly, asking American politicians to stop sending money rather than let it be abused.

While in the United States I was asked to meet a New Jersey Senator, Mr Lautenberg, in New York. I would plead with him to intervene, as many interested and worried Irish Americans wanted. The Senator was busy and it was difficult for our friends over there to arrange the interview. The best Senator Lautenberg could offer was to talk to me in his car as he was driving from his office to the airport. As soon as we got into his car and moved off he had to answer his car phone. There seemed little chance that anything would come of all this as he continued to deal with his phone calls. Relief came when we went under the Lincoln Tunnel. His phone died. During the silence I said what I wanted to say as briefly as possible. 'Give me something I can tell my constituents about', he said, 'I want rights for everybody too, but tell me something I can tell my constituents.' He was Jewish and knew what discrimination meant, but what argument could he use? 'Try this', I said. 'Your American tax dollars are being wasted in Ireland. Our message is, If you want your money wasted, waste it, but not in Ireland where we cannot stand over what is being done with it and where it is doing more harm than good. We would be better off without it unless Americans control it properly.'

That was something he could sell to his constituents and as we came out of the tunnel he did not use the phone again. There was still time to talk and as we arrived at the airport, he asked if I would come in and continue the conversation. I said 'no', I had said all I needed to say and asked his help.

Senator Lautenberg promised and kept his promise and his help was important in trying to get their money and ours used properly and not wasted on those who had enough already, leaving poor people as poor as before. He visited Ireland a number of times in the following years, encouraged by good friends like Mr and Mrs Logue of the 'Doors of Hope' in New Jersey.

Sometimes visits abroad involved a lot of meetings, sometimes separated by few hundred miles. Sometimes they involved giving evidence about discrimination or extradition to politicians or local councils or courts. I believed nobody should be extradited to a British court on a political charge, and on a criminal one only with the strongest possible safeguards. The British justice system even at its best is outdated and cumbersome, in some aspects even ridiculous. It never had to be radically reformed. The devastation of war had spared it, unlike the systems of other European countries which had to be rebuilt after the devastation of World War Two. British political and legal systems remained as they were, relics of a past age.

One of the court cases was the last day of Joe Doherty's first fight in New York against being sent back into British jurisdiction. Storms and bitter cold added to the misery of what was happening to Joe. Even in the best of conditions the courts are scenes of human misery impossible to describe, although American and continental European courts seemed to show more concern and courtesy to lawyers and witnesses than British or Irish courts where judges allow and sometimes use overbearing rudeness as a weapon.

In an Amsterdam court pleading along with Sean McBride and Bernadette McAliskey and others against the extradition of Bic McFarland and Gerry Kelly, I saw those two men led in handcuffs and could never forget the indignity of that insult any more than I could ever forget the sight of Frank Cahill gazing at me through the wire mesh of a Long Kesh cage. The court in Amsterdam was given a more complete exposition of the Irish situation, politically, militarily and socially than I had ever heard. At the end of a session reporters asked, 'What are these men doing here in this court? They are soldiers fighting a war.'

On visits to any country we tried to explain what was really happening in Ireland, not a government version of it. We owed that to people in these countries, Britain, France, Italy, Norway, who were good enough to ask us. It could be worrying and exhausting in spite of the kindness and hospitality of the people. On a visit to the United States and Canada lasting about five weeks I was getting the beginnings of a hernia, it was a cold season and there were so many meetings far apart with little time between them. One evening in the middle of what I was saying to an audience I suddenly thought, 'Why am I telling the people all this? Sure, I told it to them last night'. But I had not told them last night at all. I had told a different audience maybe two hundred miles away and now the events and the audiences and the evenings were becoming a jumble in my mind which was no longer separating one segment from another. But this was the last evening of that tour and there was nothing a good sleep would not cure.

Before these invitations I had gone to the United States three times, once with my brother Liam who loved it and remembered every moment with such humour afterwards, once with my mother who did not like it and was glad to come back home because New York was at once too fussy and too casual for her, and once, almost disastrously, to attend a conference in the University College at Amherst Boston. Among those invited to that conference in the early 1970s were Martin Smyth of the Orange Order, Sammy Smyth of the UDA, Seamus Costello of the IRSP and many others involved in politics, community or church. Transporting this crowd of people across the Atlantic and keeping us for five days, all costs paid, was an expensive operation. We were never sure who paid for it but fairly sure intelligence services were interested parties. For me it was agony.

On the way to Belfast airport for the flight out I had to get out of the car three times with an agonising pain in my back. I thought it was psychological because I did not want to go to this conference and was persuaded only after a lot of argument. On the plane to London the excruciating pain came and went; the flight over the Atlantic was awful. I stood at the back of the plane a lot of the way because that was the only way I could get relief. We went by coach from the airport to the university. This took a couple of painful hours made more miserable by an RTE man who stood behind me singing and shouting in a drunken frenzy most of the time. We should have stopped him but we were going to a conference in which we would need more politeness than reason and none of us did. I regretted that afterwards, especially when I saw him still operating in RTE, probably having forgotten the drunken crassness of that agonising journey. During the conference I spent most of the time in bed, coming down for conference sessions and meals. I shared a room with a Jesuit friend and that helped. Hot towels helped even more.

On the way home painkillers took away some of the discomfort and the frenzied drinker was either absent or silent, perhaps even sober. I stood in the plane most of the way across the Atlantic, stood in London airport waiting for the plane to Belfast, then suddenly the pain disappeared. This made me sure it had been psychological. But it was not. A few days after coming home there were signs that a kidney stone had disintegrated and left of its own accord. I could not blame the conference after all. Maybe I could blame the British soldiers and their guns beating my back. Or maybe it was just nature or an act of God.

The Boston conference did not come to any conclusions. In those days it was considered good just to bring people of different political ideas together in a neutral environment. They might just as usefully have talked together in beautiful Upper Buckna, the most useful thing being that political people could see and treat each other with respect. The sharpest intelligence present was that of Seamus Costello, one of the most acutely intelligent revolutionary thinkers in Ireland. His mind was sharp, his memory efficient and his ability to marshal his thoughts into scintillating argument superb. On one occasion during the Boston conference he spoke in response to Martin Smyth. It was like a brilliant fencing master performing after an exhibition of elephant riding.

The loyalist unionists there, Sammy Smyth, Andy Tyrie and others, recognised Seamus Costello's political and debating talent and we had no doubt that he was docketed in some minds as a potential enemy whose future would soon be anxiously discussed by loyalists and intelligence operators at home.

Sammy Smyth had a mind of a different kind, had a good memory and a keen interest in education, was a spokesman for the UDA and favoured decision making in society being devolved as far down the line as possible. Like Seamus Costello, he was shot dead some years later.

16

Conway Mill

In 1983 Conway Mill down the road, vacant since about 1974, became available and a local committee got it first on rent and then fully owned, about a hundred thousand square feet of industrially usable space in shocking condition. We wanted to make it into a project with work, education, cultural events on one site. We knew the British government might well send in the troops and take this over as they had taken over the Whiterock Industrial Estate, so we tried to make sure that if or when they did, concerned people in countries abroad would know about it and maybe help us. The British government did not do that but they did nearly everything else to destroy it.

They boycotted it, refused financial help, sent the troops to harass people inside and outside the premises, created a propaganda campaign which dubbed the Mill, which was set to create more than 200 jobs, a front for the IRA. We had to sue a TV company which tried to destroy the Mill through its absurd 'Cooke Report' and it probably cost them about a million pounds to defend themselves. That legal battle lasted over five years.

Such destructiveness was encouraged by some nationalist and other politicians and by the apathy of the churches that refused to accept that this was a peaceful initiative they should support. The only interest official Christians showed at the beginning was to send in a delegation to find out if a play we hosted in the buildings had a scene with bare bottoms. As far as I know it did not, but I did not bother to find out. If they were not interested in a project which could produce 200 to 250 jobs, we need not worry about their interest in bare bottoms. Eventually they would have enough to inquire about when nearly all the TV companies would be exhibiting bare bottoms almost every day, but that was not to bother them until the nineties.

The man who first saw the potential of Conway Mill was Tom Cahill, a brother of Joe and Frank. It was agreed that one of our nine available floors should be dedicated to education and so the Conway Enterprises and the Conway Education Project began. In 2003 one of our Management Committee asked that the name Conway should be deleted from the Mill's name and documents. This was because Conway was a pirate who lived by theft and the street the Mill was in had been named after him by the City Fathers. He thought it deserved better than that and so did we all.

After more than twenty years of effort, toil, boycott, neglect and attempts to destroy it, Conway Mill in 2004 came near to putting together the financial package we needed to develop the site as what we believed would be a landmark project for the development of the whole area of west Belfast. In the nineteen seventies we had dreamed of an education project which would be independent, financially supported by a commercial operation. I had seen the like elsewhere, like one in Lausanne in which big supermarkets created and sustained an education project. But that was not free enough. Conway Mill seemed like fulfilling the dream, one hundred thousand square feet of space, one floor for education, an education project upheld by a commercial venture, over all of which the people working and the people learning would have control. No wonder there were people who wanted to eliminate it. Friends in the Shankill Road, including UDA people, were sympathetic, more sympathetic than others who claimed respectability by avoiding people like us. For years Conway Mill was the only place in town where all political parties were invited to come and be heard and be talked to. Most of them accepted the invitation. That did not stop the propaganda against it; it may even have made it worse. Nor did it stop one of our directors having a bomb placed under his car, which fortunately only partly exploded. By 2004 people were hopeful that Conway Mill was at last taking its proper place in our community. For years as a mill it had been a private enterprise in which workers, especially women, suffered. Now it was to be an integrated site where work, enterprise, independence, culture, education would be in the one place, where you could go to work in the same building as the theatre, where you could have education alongside people building up their enterprises.

With a scepticism which was not natural but only the result of long seeing how those with power protected power, I would believe the effectiveness of the package when it was on the table. And at that point, at the age of eighty years of age, it would be time for me to go, and to watch people who obviously knew their business get on with it.

17

Learning the Lessons

At one time and another I was on management committees of more limited companies than any of my friends, but none of the companies made a profit. Springhill Community House was one, the Open College another, the Ulster People's College another, Conway Enterprises, Conway Education, Whiterock Industrial Estate.

I was not any use at managing and when projects got going I wanted to leave them so that others would do it right. I had a horror of projects being clericalised, another of projects having people clinging on to them after their useful days were over; some businesses had had that trouble when I was growing up in Belfast. It seemed right to help get something going if you could, and then make way for somebody else. That was sometimes interpreted as leaving the rising ship but no matter, our community had to be not only demilitarised but declericalised and made efficient as well.

Priests had founded cooperatives and worked for human rights and all of us had reason to be proud of that; still a priest was not ordained for business or management. But for all this high idealism I found myself still doing things at seventy-plus which I should have left off doing years before.

One of the curious things about the north of Ireland, and Belfast in particular, from the nineteen seventies on was the number of business projects the government put into the hands of clergy and others who were not business people and who indeed had turned their backs on business as a way of life for themselves. It seemed like an extension of the policy of inbuilt inefficiency in our society.

Government seemed to avoid putting money for development in our area into the hands of business people, and instead gave huge sums to committees consisting of clergy, or teachers, or lawyers and such, all of whom had turned their backs on business as a way of life for themselves. It is like financing a school and putting everybody in to run it except teachers. The government was investing for safety and public opinion, not for development. So there was good reason for giving what little help you could to set up working projects and then clearing out and leaving people who had taken business or trade as their way of life to get on with it.

The situation in West Belfast became more and more ridiculous as millions of pounds said to be for development of business were administered by non-business people. So the team in Springhill Community House went out one day and put leaflets into as many shops as we could up and down our area. Until we did this we did not realise how many small shops there were. These were business people who had kept money flowing in the area through so many years. Our small traders had provided the necessities of life in their front of the road, corner and back street shops. And yet they were being told in effect that if there was money for development of trade and commerce, for the creation of wealth, it was to be put into the hands of anyone but business people.

Our leaflets made an appeal to the business people to see to it that if capital was coming in it was they who should be getting and using it. We asked them to come to a meeting in the hope that a Traders' Association would emerge. In the old days my father and his companions graduated from apprenticeship into trades unions and debating societies, and then into negotiators and leaders of their own Vintners' Association. The traders in West Belfast could have a society powerful enough to save investment money from running down politically safe but commercially unproductive drains. It was a very small meeting. Perhaps the traders were as demoralised as many other people were and perhaps the struggle to keep going and surviving was enough for them. But a Traders' Association was formed and members of the Springhill team organised it until the traders were in a position to let them go. And they did go, as usual. The association went on its way and soon other traders' associations followed in North, South and East Belfast working together.

Those who controlled resources in our society seemed to believe that people who were actually making a living in our community were not capable of making a better living for themselves and should not be encouraged or helped to do so. They refused also to recognise that however welcome investment from outside may be, foreign enterprises will help create a stable successful economy only if they come into a community based on local people's enterprise. If there is a sound local trading and manufacturing base then the inevitable departure of foreign firms for bigger profits elsewhere is less of a shock to the system. And in any case, if a community is thriving by its own efforts, it will all the more quickly adapt to new needs when new work arrives from outside.

The British government was forced to pour money into areas like ours because it was criticised in Ireland and abroad for not doing it. But when they did pour it in, they made sure it would not produce local wealth and thus reduce local dependency.

Their improvident subsidising of failing industry reached dangerous levels, and dependency increased with it. If an enterprise like De Lorean arrived it got as much as it wanted and more than it needed, possibly ending in failure, while local entrepreneurs were refused capital on the ground that the risks would be too great. The risk with De Lorean could not have been greater – there were few in Belfast who had real hopes for it from the start – and West Belfast could have been richly developed on the money that was wasted on this and much else like it.

The two ideals of continuing education for everybody and locally based work as well as investment from outside were attractive to us but not for government and that was what our non-profit taking limited companies were about. In the south by the nineteen eighties there was a growing awareness that international investment had to be paralleled by financial support for native industries. In the north there was no such understanding as far as we could see. Local educational and wealth creating enterprises found it hard to survive. But people tried to create learning and work and independence nevertheless.

People in our neighbourhood created a lot of events to try to encourage realistic public discussion, not only about themselves but about us all. We could only use the BBC and RTE with caution, if at all. Since 1975 I had not heard from UTV. Then during the nineteen eighties BBC and RTE had censorship more severe than anything since the Second World War. In order to give some appearance of balance they often reached out for some of us who would give a nationalist or republican view of current affairs. The people we elected to do this were forbidden by law to broadcast and RTE not only obeyed the law but asked for even greater censorship. For a long while I had been doing programmes, some religious, some commenting on current affairs and some cultural, about films, books, plays. It was pleasant but I became less and less willing to be used as a substitute for the people elected to speak on our behalf about political events. I wrote to BBC and RTE and said I wanted to do no more of it and was opting out. Some time later a BBC producer told people they had stopped inviting me because I had become too testy. Like much else in broadcasting it was untrue.

People like our neighbours had to find alternative ways of making their opinions known, as they had a right to do. The list of discussion events they invented or helped to invent in the past fifty years is impressive and perhaps unique.

One of them was an International Conference to discuss the future of democracy in Ireland. That was in 1990. It was held downtown in the posh Europa Hotel. It took another few years before the government allowed us to march to our own City Hall, so the choice of venue was our political statement that as citizens we would go anywhere we wished competently and proudly. Delegates from sixteen countries came. Press reporters came too but most of their newspapers ignored it. Some years later we organised conferences in Belfast and Dublin to discuss Democratising the Churches and most of the media people ignored those also although they had often complained that the churches should act more democratically. When we published a word for word report of the two church conferences a woman architect reviewing it in a religious magazine asked a question like the one asked about Jesus Christ: 'Can any good come out of West Belfast?' Jesus had summed it up: your opponents may well be those who should be of your own household.

I can think of no community in Belfast which has done so much to understand, define and suggest remedies for their problems and to propose plans for their future prosperity. But at the end of it all –the ground breaking public inquiries, the constant new forms of discussion, the repeated invitations to people of all kinds to come and talk, their new experiments in education and theatre and much else besides – the struggle for power and control still went on and as far a possible the strugglers left West Belfast and such people out of account.

While the government was still refusing to help us develop Conway Mill community associations in our district paid my way to Washington in 1994 for a conference to encourage trade and industrial investment in Ireland. I went to Washington with a load of pamphlets about the Conway boycott in the hope that we could again draw attention to a financial scandal in which American dollars were used or refused for local political reasons.

I did not want to go. Apart from being tired, round the seventy mark and not wanting to make more big journeys than necessary – the cancer operation was still three years ahead – there was a new generation of young people coming along well able to oppose cruelty abroad and create industry at home. It did not need old fellows like me. But Conway Mill was important for our future prosperity and the more voices saying that the better, even tired, ageing ones.

I did not need the pamphlets after all. Just as we gathered for a meeting in Washington, it was announced that the London administration had lifted the boycott on the Mill. This lifting of the boycott was misinterpreted by many people at home who assumed the Mill had got government help for development at last. But it had not, and a long time was to pass before it did, and even then the enormous sum of anything from one and half to four million pounds to provide modern conditions for the workers already there and the 200 workers we hoped for in the future would still be refused. Since we could have developed the Mill and much else with the money government departments had squandered in West Belfast, this waste should have been seen as just as big a scandal as anything revealed later in the Dublin tribunals, but waste and misuse of money were so ingrained in northern society that it was considered normal.

At the Washington conference we were surprised at how forthcoming the US Secretary for Trade, Mr. Brown, was. He must have known – his people had reason to know – what discrimination and industrial cruelty were about. But he also had the interests of employers in mind. He urged three good reasons for Americans to invest in the north of Ireland: our people spoke English, they were good workers and their labour would cost at least 25 per cent less than in America. We saw it differently; we could see good reason for our people offering bargains to anyone wanting to use our labour or facilities, but creating a permanent low-wage economy should not be on the agenda.

Already at a press conference with a senior Catholic and a senior Presbyterian churchman we had said it was unreal to invite anyone to invest in Ireland unless they could be sure of value for their money. It was much the same as the argument used with Senator Lautenberg: we cannot stand over anything in Ireland in which American money or anybody else's is wasted. We asked, 'Since it is wrong to ask Americans to invest money by siting industry in the north of Ireland unless they get value for money, will the churches ensure that the practice of hiring people because of their religion and membership of religious societies rather than their ability will cease? Otherwise we are inviting people to waste money through the same inefficiency that has crippled us already.'

There was a hesitant admission from the Presbyterian church spokesman that indeed there had been some problems and no doubt something was being done about them and more would doubtless be done in the future. It was not admitted that the inefficiency resulting largely from church-bound secret societies was one of the reasons why so much in the northeast had withered from relative prosperity to relative non-productivity during the past seventy years.

At the last session of the Washington conference Inez McCormack of the union Unison raised the question of a low-wage economy. We had received a dull lecture from a representative of Shorts Brothers of Belfast, now Bombardier, which sounded like an address to shareholders at an annual general meeting of the company, about how the prosperity of Northern Ireland would evolve very largely from the success of Shorts/Bombardier. Inez said that if anyone was thinking of creating a low-wage economy in Ireland this would be unwelcome. I said we were just coming out of a 30 years war and we wanted peace, and if it was being suggested that our future prosperity was going to depend on our making weapons to visit the same misery on others as we had experienced, this would be as unwelcome as the idea of a low-wage economy. A senior clergyman on the dais then made the distinction between weapons for defence and weapons for offence and thus justified the arms trade we were supposed to embrace. It was daunting to realise that after all these years of war people, including religious leaders, were telling us we must stop using arms to protect ourselves and get to making arms for use against others and if we did not, prosperity might elude us. Later that dilemma came to Derry where by a strange irony a Nobel Peace Prize winner encouraged investment by Raytheon, makers of software for missile systems, and the churches which had demanded that weapons be laid aside would stand silently by while their parishioners and congregations would help to make them.

It was an old dilemma, but one scarcely talked about because of the respectability which Christians attach to arms in the 'right' hands. Christians in Belfast were forced to look for jobs in Shorts/Bombardier, forced even to demand them as a matter of equality when, if all Christians had stood together against the arms trade, they would have been demanding that the arms factory be taken away and something decent put in its place.

But we Christians in Belfast were often vague about what we were doing, even to ourselves. For decades workers in Shorts were told to allow only a handful of Catholics in and they did this as a duty to God and Ulster. Then Shorts was sold. Shortly after that I met a Protestant cleric and said to him, ' Do you not think it strange that your people went into Shorts on a Friday determined to keep the Catholics out and then went in the following Monday morning only to find they were now working for Catholics?' Bombardier, who got Shorts almost as a gift, were said to be practising Catholics. I thought the irony of that situation would persuade him to talk about how all of us were being used.

He looked at me for a moment. 'No', he said, 'I don't think about things like that; that is politics'. Once again an effort to talk with a fellow Christian about the realities of bad government, big business, exploitation and multiple exclusions died a swift death. Maybe religious people do not appreciate ironies.

Cardinal Tomás Ó Fiaich did. He also recognised the realities of our situation and the difficulty of changing it. Personal goodwill was overcome by institutionalised refusal of it. Once when there was serious trouble in the prisons he and Archbishop Armstrong of the Church of Ireland were in London together. When they arrived back in Belfast, reporters asked them what they thought should be done about the allegations that prisoners were assaulted and abused. Tomás Ó Fiaich was forthright as usual and said it was wrong. Archbishop

Armstrong hesitated and then said these were serious matters which he agreed should be investigated. Both went home to their episcopal houses in Armagh. Tomás Ó Fiaich slept soundly that night but Archbishop Armstrong was distressed into the small hours by phone calls from local members of the freemasons and other societies indignant at what he had said, little though it was. Next day Armstrong made a new statement in which he practically retracted what he had said the day before. He was an open friendly man, but he knew where the power lay in the north of Ireland and how vulnerable the Protestant clergy were to it. Until they dismantle the power of these societies the influence of benign Protestant clergy cannot flourish.

One day in the nineteen eighties an official phoned and asked me to dinner. I courteously declined dinner – it is too hard to talk and eat dinner at the same time; you can't whistle and chaw meal – so I said I would call over for coffee. He told me Derek (not his real name) would be there as well.

I did not ask who this Derek was because I had been talking to a local politician of that name a few days before and assumed it was he. I was surprised then when I arrived at the official's house and found not this friend but a high-ranking British army officer. I had met him already some years before. We talked about the political situation. During the conversation I said the British government would never solve its problems or ours until it stopped pretending their armed republican opponents in Ireland were thugs and criminals. To my surprise Derek said, 'We know we are not just dealing with thugs and criminals'. 'But', I said, 'that is what you are saying, that the republicans are thugs and criminals, instead of admitting the truth about what is happening here.' 'No', he said. 'That is what the government is saying; it is not what the army is telling our government.'

Our host had not said much so far but now he said, 'You have to remember that what the army tells the government about the situation and what the government tells the people about it may be two quite different things.'

In other words the British government knew the truth about the conflict because its own army was telling it. But the general public and the foot soldiers in the streets – many of whom, like the police, suffered nervous breakdowns through what they were ordered to do in Ireland – believed what their government told them. And what their government told them was different from what their army leaders were telling the government. Derek said calmly that the IRA was a highly motivated, politically astute and very efficient military force. So part of the problem then was a government fighting a war armed with lies. That being so, the government could not win and their army knew it. A short while later they publicly admitted it.

Eventually, when involved in a much bigger war in Iraq, the London government showed how lying was not just part but a vital part of their normal method of waging war.

No doubt there were people in the British military and police who were honest and genuinely wanted peace and good government. After all, as clerics we had believed our church institutions could solve problems too, even at the very moment when some were creating them. But the political machine in which state officials worked deliberately corrupted what they had to say and do. Bad people doing bad things was easy to understand if you really believed bad people existed. But the worst evil came when good people were persuaded to do bad things. That was one of the most frightening aspects of our whole affair. An institution that persuades evil-minded people to do bad things is only doing what you would expect. An institution that persuades good people to do cruel things is one of the most frightening monsters on earth. That is one reason for being afraid of armies and police and financial institutions, and parties and governments and any other institution. They have a latent ability to make good people do evil while publicly offering to make evil people do good, and we have to do more than pray to stop that latent ability awakening. Some day we will turn our thinking about all our institutions upside down and look at them more critically and realistically.

What Derek said that evening made clear that governments did not believe their own propaganda. But unfortunately many of those who issue the propaganda in their name do. We learned how corrosive and persuasive propaganda could be and how decent people could be willingly deceived by it.

We were standing in a line in front of Belfast City Hall silently protesting against the abuse and unjust imprisonment of Roisin McAliskey when a man approached, read our placards, stood beyond speaking distance and shouted, ' Get away out of that and go and find work'. He pretended to believe the unionist propaganda that Catholics do not work. Along the line of picketers were students, workers, retired workers, voluntary workers; there was not one person in that line who did not have a history of work. The self-satisfied little man staring and shouting at us did not try to find out by talking to us. Unionist slogans were his weapon and it did not much matter whether he believed in them or not. It was useless to talk to a man whose one purpose is to insult you, not to converse with you. But no matter.

As the twentieth century ended with ceasefires our political hopes rose and at the same time our clerical morale went down. Scandals we never foresaw erupted in the church. We knew what could happen to a church; we did not know what actually was happening.

What happened in the past, when the church was taken over by scoundrels, we had studied in our history lectures in Maynooth, but we understood that that was all over. One day after a lecture a fellow student said we all assumed papal and other church scandals were a thing of the past, but how did we know they were? We had the word of authorities and officials for it. It was like our belief in the impartiality of the BBC and the excellence of the Irish Times; we knew about these because the BBC and the Irish Times told us. In neither case did we have any proof. We need not assume that on the ground or on high things were as sound in the church as we were told. We just hoped they were.

Things had often happened which caused embarrassment. A priest maybe got into trouble, a crude way of saying he had fallen in love. He would possibly be told to go off somewhere else, perhaps to America. This had to do with the preachers' doctrine of 'the occasions of sin'. If, so said the doctrine, you get people away from their present occasions of sin, or temptations, or inducements, this is more than half the battle. They still have their own thoughts and acquisitiveness to deal with but to get clear of the present occasions of sin, the things and people ensnaring them, was at least a good start. A priest at the poker table, or having the pages turned for him at the piano by a pretty girl, or dancing, or visiting too much in the one place was perhaps getting into an occasion of sin. If he got into trouble, the cure was first of all to move him away from those occasions of sin, homely and attractive as they were – exile for his own safety, a harsh but uncomplicated and even innocent view of how our minds work. Years hence we will look back and wonder at how scandalously cruel we could be to exile a man because he was lonely.

When news of more serious scandals emerged about abuse of children people asked why something more than exile or shifting about was not done about it, saying it was a futile gesture to move priests or teachers or any others from one place to another when they had a condition which was going to go with them wherever they went. We had not realised that the trouble was less with the external occasions of sin and more with the internal instincts which were so difficult to control. You carried your own occasions of sin around with you wherever you went. So moving from place to place did not solve the problems; it just shifted them around. But we did not realise that. As problems unfolded and we saw how deeply troubled the church really was, we had to realise it.

Church officials honestly tried to solve problems the only way they knew. Jesus on his cross said, 'Forgive them; they don't know what they are doing'. The people who created the scandals knew what they were doing; the people trying to solve them did not. The frightening impulses of those who abuse are still waiting to be studied properly.

When the news came out one morning in 1992 that Bishop Eamon Casey had had a child and not acknowledged it, this was a simple fact, not an earthquake and fellow clerics saw it as such. If a man makes arrangements for his and another's sexual comfort, we may not agree with what he does but he may do little harm if he treats people with respect. The biggest problem some of us had with Eamon was his millionaire lifestyle. And while he did a lot of good things, most of them were for countries abroad and like most of the bishops he left us in the north alone. That was a pity because lives could have been saved by individuals as dynamic as Casey and groups as influential as the bishops if they had taken a firm stand for our safety.

What would have happened if Eamon had come out and faced the people in his Cathedral in Galway and told them he had fathered a child? It is possible they would have said he should treat his partner and child with respect and preach accordingly. And they might have asked him to stay. Every person in the church can make his or her own arrangements for companionship but the heart of the problem is that anybody in a relationship of intimacy similar to that of man and wife should be able to say publicly, 'This is my wife. This is my husband'. It is unjust that men and women should have to love each other by stealth, if friends are turned into worried fugitives.

The questions Dutch Catholics asked in the nineteen sixties should be asked and answered in public discussion in Ireland now. The right to marry is such a basic human right that one wonders more and more how a church can forbid anyone to marry. It could say that if a priest marries he is no longer acceptable as a serving priest. But however imprudent that is, it is not the same as saying his marriage is invalid. The real issues about celibacy and marriage in the Catholic church need to be addressed in Ireland, no matter what policy the Vatican adopts.

Having for years gone to social study and other conferences and meetings and given retreats for priests and having been honoured so many times by their confidence, I had every reason to believe that very little was wrong with us. The vast majority of priests I knew were decent men for whom hard work and a lot of worry were their biggest concerns. Even when I was doing and saying things that fellow priests wondered about or disapproved of, I remember only very few of them showing unpleasantness to me. When a fellow priest gets into trouble, perhaps even brought to court or to prison, the sense of tragedy and sadness among fellow priests is great and lasting. They need the help of each other and of those in positions of power in the church.

And we need a response from leaders worthy of a church with two thousand years experience of what human beings can do, and of what enlightened human wisdom can do for us when we bring trouble on ourselves.

When the child abuse scandals appeared, church officials rushed to assure state authorities that we should all report every instance of suspected child abuse at once to the police or welfare authorities. This was not as helpful as it seemed. Priests are strong-minded people who have to listen to things of all kinds from people of all kinds. They value confidentiality and are valued for it. If they should report every time they came across abuse what then was to become of the priest as an adviser anyone could go to in trouble? A man or woman who had suddenly allowed him or herself to do something of which they were later ashamed could not come to a priest any more because he would be obliged to tell someone else. The priest as advisor, counsellor, rescuer from the cliff edge, was disappearing. Some of us made the point to officials as that crisis developed but it made no difference. There was more than a hint of panic which ill became us.

18

Way Out

After seventy years with no major health problems I was surprised when told I had cancer. My father died with cancer at 59, but his father lived to be 102 and my mother lived to 85, and so at the age of 70, I probably had a few years left. But pains are pains and good doctors are good doctors and x-rays cannot lie so I asked the surgeon to tell me the worst possible thing first and then the best thing and found myself somewhere in between. Visiting Donegal and going round the garden was like saying goodbye to old friends in case I might not see them again. And in spite of all my efforts to keep a good face forward and remember what reality is all about, my head was taking fallback positions whether I liked them or not, positions abandoned one by one. Something in the bowel? Well, it might be just an irritation. Well no, it's a growth. Oh well, it may be benign. No, it's malignant. Your mind goes into automatic, thinks for you and goes through all the possibilities beginning with the worst, going back to the best and starting with the worst all over again. Sometimes you persuade yourself to stop thinking about it altogether.

But what would have killed you a few years ago can be dealt with now. And at this time we were just crossing over the conversational barrier behind which we talked about 'The Big C' and beginning to talk openly about cancer if you had it. While my mind was working on its fallback positions it suddenly stopped in its tracks when I got to the hospital ward for admission. Going into hospital is never pleasant and no operation is easy. Having to wait five minutes and not having brought a book and not being able to resist reading things, I read the notices on the big board outside the ward.

'What to do about your Cancer'. 'The Ulster Cancer Society.' 'How to look after your water works.' It seemed as if the notices had nothing to do with anything but cancer. Nor had they. I wondered if this ward was for anything else, because if not, your fallback positions were demolished once you got there.

Ten days later, after the operation and once more enjoying the expertise and kindness of other people I mentioned this notice board to a nurse. Would it not be a bit upsetting for, say, a young man leaving wife or family and hoping he does not have cancer to come on such an array of notices which might suggest he probably had?

She did not agree. Those notices, she said, are for the staff, not for you and you should not be reading them. I doubted that, but having escaped so neatly and resolving from now on to lead a good contention-free life, why should I argue?

Going back into the Mater Hospital as a patient where I had been a chaplain nearly fifty years before was like coming back to where I started. It made me feel my age more than ever and how quickly we pass through a world where everything is more permanent than we are. The great doors to the wards were the same doors as fifty years ago, the floors the same, I thought the lockers were the same but they weren't. The holy statues were gone and so were the nursing nuns. More people of different religious and political persuasions were working there, even loyalist devotees. No more communal prayers said in the wards; if you wanted prayers you said them privately in bed or publicly in the chapel. And on the Sunday morning when you were too sore or too tired to get up, the chaplain coming round to share the Eucharist with you was a nun.

I wanted to tell people I had been a chaplain there nearly fifty years ago, to talk about the Saturday night hops in the Extern and the doings of the young doctors and medical students who became such pillars of respectability afterwards, but it did not seem interesting to anybody any more.

In two minds about whether I wanted a chaplain to visit me, and shamefully remembering how callow and brash and naive I had been, I remembered an Englishman who came to work with us in the seventies, determinedly English, ex-British army, wanting to help but hard to convince that his government had really behaved as badly as it did in Ireland. Fresh from the Catholic Renewal Movement, he got a heart attack in Belfast. He went into a hospital and all was well. When he came out he talked about how the chaplain had annoyed him, worse, had bored him. So when he went into hospital again he said he would not register himself as a Catholic or any of its many branches, Protestant or other. So as what then? As a Moravian Orthodox Uniate. They can't have a chaplain for that, he said happily.

Lying in his hospital bed some days later he seemed exhausted and no happier. He groaned. 'I put myself down as a Moravian Orthodox Uniate.' 'Good. Well?' 'They had never heard of Moravian Orthodox Uniates.' 'And so...?' 'And so all the blooming chaplains came talking to me!'

When you are getting old and sometimes feeling guilty, people ask and you ask yourself, 'If you had it to do again, would you do the same things the same way?' There is no real answer to that and we have to be content with Brian Smeaton's when he worked with us in Belfast: 'We did the best we could with the information we had at the time'.

So, yes, we probably would do much the same things in much the same way. Still, I wish we had taken a stronger stand against some of the unproductive nonsense we put up with. We should have been tougher and worked harder to dismantle the fear that makes people hide inside their own minds. In the mid-seventies we set up an organisation called Platform and our first public conference was about fear because we believed fear was the most pervasive and damaging characteristic of our society. Take it away and real change will follow. People were afraid of other people and of too many things and this fear was carefully and cunningly fostered by people who wanted power. Someone said, real freedom for people begins not when they all stand up together and say, 'We believe this' but when one stands up and says, 'I don't believe that'. Our safety always depended too much on our being compliant, our jobs, respectability, even at times our lives. One false move and you could lose any or all of them. One honest move could lose them too. But there are many sides to our story and running parallel with political, religious and economic chicanery are kindness, quiet respect and goodness which I and many people like me experienced in great measure.

So perhaps together, not just as individuals, we could have taken a stronger line against fear, exploitation and unproductive nonsense.

Nowadays we are all making new definitions of practically everything, of business, economics, religion, politics, morality, drama, vegetable growing and of the morality of keeping people unhappily bound to where industrialists want them while moving animals miserably around all over the world.

We have learned a lot of lessons through trial and success as well as through trial and error. Having learned enough lessons, now we have to create freedom for us all to experiment with our new ideas. That pleasant task could last to the end of time and I know only two reasons that would make me glad to live for ever in this world. One is to enjoy the beautiful things of the world like you see standing with friends on a bridge across the Ray River in Donegal looking towards Muckish; the other is that it would give me time to put all the lessons I learned into practice.

And maybe we really could change the world after all.

APPENDIX I
Letter to Bishop William Philbin 1971

Although the position of priests is described in terms of their being co-workers with Bishops and sharing the priesthood of Jesus Christ the laws under which priests live and work make clear another element in the relationship. This appears in the laws which most closely govern the private life of priests. For instance, it is laid down in canon law that clerics shall be closely supervised in the frequency of their confessions, their prayer and even examination of conscience, also in what they wear - canon 136 lays down the form of dress, forbidding even the use of a ring on the finger - and there are penalties for failure to observe the laws.

Even the priests' personal goods and money are not entirely at their own disposal (e.g.canon 137), their leisure time is subject to law (canons 138 - 140) and strict limits are placed upon where they can go and what they can do.

The point is made not because these are bad prescriptions but because they are matters about which normally a professional man can be trusted to use his own discretion. Professional men have unwritten rules which they obey. The existence of such laws in the code of canon law seems a judgement on the inability of priests to maintain proper standards without being compelled to do so, a judgement which runs counter to the thought of the Vatican Council document on priests which recognises their maturity and responsibility. An interesting aspect of this is that no other body of men, or women, nowadays is bound by such laws. The nearest one can come to such a strict control on the dress, manners and leisure activity of people is the rules which were imposed upon domestics and living-in workers in the past e.g. workers who lived with their employers in Belfast in the early years of this century were closely supervised in their free time, dress, entertainment of friends etc. There seems to be no other kind of parallel for the laws mentioned.

This impression is reinforced by the canon law which forbids the cleric to 'leave his diocese for a notable time' or which presumes him to be living in concubinage if he does not accept the ruling of the Ordinary that he does not visit or have in his house women who may cause scandal. It is not that the present prescriptions are not good, it is that among professional men it would be taken for granted that such things could be left to the discretion of the men concerned; such laws are made for those who are presumed not to have sufficient responsibility to arrange matters decently.

The Maynooth Statutes, although they soften the tone of some of the laws found in the general canon law, make a provision (No 15) which would prevent a priest from going on a journey even with his own mother or sister, in order to avoid scandal. Here the law forbids something which is normally proper and necessary. When a law requires that a priest wears clean clothes, prescribes the hour beyond which he may not play cards, prescribes that he wear a hat, forbids him to smoke in public streets, again the matter of the laws may be wise and beneficial but to find a parallel to such laws being imposed on a body of men, one has to look to the conditions of service of domestics and living-in workers.

It is with this in mind that one has to understand the assertion that in the attitude of the legislators to priests there is to be found the idea that priests are indeed in some way in similar status to servants. One of the ways in which the Vatican Council could have helped priests would have been to have some adjustment made to the laws. No such attempt was made, although some of those attending the Vatican Council showed awareness of the problem. For example, such awareness of the existence of a problem was shown by Bishop Guyot, President of the French Episcopal Commission for the Clergy, who said:

'What many priests want today is that their relations with Bishops should be in a climate of mutual confidence. They want to be able to express with full frankness their hopes and difficulties, to exchange experiences, to propose possible concrete solutions, to take certain initiatives. In other words our priests do not want simply to have the duty of carrying out decisions from above, they want to take part in the working out of the pastoral task in a diocese. They want to have a presence at the evolving of the work so that they really will be able to co-operate later on.......with very great mutual generosity. The Bishop and his Priests run the risk of proceeding along parallel ways which only meet at infinity - which, as everyone knows, is from the pastoral point of view, too late ! '

That some adjustment of relationships is necessary is becoming increasingly clear. The Osservatore Romano said, in relation to present controversies: 'Soldiers in the past war obeyed the orders of their officers without knowing the strategy of the great chiefs and the tactics of their immediate superiors. Why therefore should the divine authority of the pastors of the Church not demand a similar submission in the sphere of faith and morals?'

To place those subject to authority in the church in the same category as soldiers is a way of expressing a relationship which seems unfortunate and excluded by the Vatican Council document on Priests. Recently too Archbishop O Boyle said that those priests who did not submit to the recent ruling in Humanae Vitae 'should go and find a pope and a church of their own'. Here again, one does not question the rights of those in authority or the duties of those bound by it, but when one considers that this implies that a priest can be cut off from the work he has been doing for years, and left - as has been made clear for instance in Southwark - without means and without home if this should be considered desirable, the only parallel one can find for this is in a master-servant relationship which is no longer found in secular affairs where the right of dismissal is being more and more restricted and dismissal itself is becoming less and less punitive.

That the relationships between priests and others is in need of serious consideration and perhaps adjustment may be seen from two incidents in our own circumstances. Here a serious deterioration is evident. Some years ago it would have been considered monstrous if a priest were publicly rebuked and humiliated in front of his parishioners. It would have been considered equally monstrous for a priest to have to submit to the indignity of acquainting his people with his own faults from his own pulpit. Nowadays these things can be and have been done. Clearly then the relationship of priests to those who have authority over them cannot be presumed to be that which the Vatican Council envisaged.

Similarly, it is clearly wrong that a priest should have been - not rebuked which would have been understandable - but abused in language which a few years ago we were accustomed to exhort people not to use because it was an abuse of God's gift of speech and a grave offence against a brother in Christ. That this should be done by a Vicar General in the name of a bishop reveals the presence of standards which as a priest one finds it increasingly difficult to share and sympathise with. One finds it particularly anomalous in a world which is rapidly coming to understand that not even servants would be subjected to verbal abuse.

It may very well be that the opinion that the relationship of priests to other members of the church is not in need of consideration and possibly of adjustment, and that it is wrong to find certain elements in the relationships which suggest a lowering of the dignity of priests. The suggestion has been made that in order to find out, and possibly to avert what is potentially a very difficult and damaging situation in which we could very well lose priests whom we can ill afford to lose, a Commission of Priests should be set up to examine every aspect of the life and work of priests in our country and our diocese. This is a suggestion which may well merit serious consideration. The priests in Ireland are by no means immune from the difficulties which priests have suffered elsewhere and unless there is recognition of the fact that relationships between priests and those in authority is in some places a most grave problem which weighs heavily on the minds of many priests, we shall suffer similar losses, losses which are all the more tragic because they could have been prevented.

APPENDIX II
Statment to the Priests Council 1971

The Vatican Council document on priests emphasised among other things the maturity and responsibility of priests as well as their dignity. This document outlined a relationship between priests and bishops in which authority and respect both find a place and which ought to be a norm towards which we should work.

However, there are certain indications that this healthy relationship of brothers in Christ working together in harmony cannot be presumed to exist already and cannot,where it does not exist already, be brought about without efforts on the part of all of us.

The relationship of respect, for authority on the one hand and for responsibility and maturity on the other, is not the relationship envisaged in the law which governs priests. It may be hoped that in any revision of canon law and local statutes these should begin to express a better relationship than they do at present. Some of the laws under which priests live and work do not recognise fully their maturity or their personal responsibility. For men who exercise so responsible a ministry it should not be necessary to supervise as closely as the law envisages such matters as the dress which priests wear, the small details of their private lives or even their prayer life. In order to achieve a tolerable relationship bishops do not insist too closely upon the duties of supervision with which the law burdens them. Laws which are seen to be undesirable should be revised and there is a good case therefore for priests to request that this should be done and that any revision of canon law should include the outlining of a relationship between bishops and clergy which is more in keeping with the spirit of the Vatican Council's document on the matter. This relationship is that of cooperators with the father of the flock, of priests with the fatherly representative of Jesus Christ Our Lord. The relationship envisaged in the canon law is nearer to one of master and servant and does not reflect either the desirable situation or the situation as it exists when bishops and priests are in harmony with each other.

One of the major problems which will face us in the future will be that of the existing relations between priests and those in authority. In these difficult times we cannot leave such important matters to chance in the hope that everything will happen as we wish it to happen. There has not been for many years a crisis among priests similar to that which we are experiencing today. And neither in Ireland as a whole nor in this diocese are we immune from it. Priests need all the help and understanding they can be given. It is very saddening and very frightening too, to hear the comments of priests and to realise that there is a considerable disquiet amounting to resentment being experienced in some quarters because it is felt that they are not being treated with the consideration that is their due.

Priests must be reassured that if for example they are unfortunate because of sickness or old age they will be provided for. They must be assured too that if they commit any fault they will still be treated with dignity. It is not right that a priest should be for example subjected to indignity in front of members of his parishioners, or be addressed, whatever faults he may be seen to have committed, in abusive language. And yet these things have happened among us in recent times. That they should happen is wrong. That they should pass without vigorous comment is a sign that our standard of acceptable behaviour towards each other is lower than the charity of Our Lord Jesus Christ would demand of us.

We all need to give an example of charity and justice to each other and those in authority have a special obligation to show mercy and love and justice as well as temperance and humility to all with whom they deal. Any of us can only make a personal assessment of whether we do carry out these duties or not. I think it is an unhappy fact that we have much to reproach ourselves for in so many ways. I think also that unless we seriously face the many problems of relationships with each other in this diocese as everywhere else we shall first alienate and then lose some of our priests and some of our best lay people. And it is worth remarking if an average of two priests were eventually to leave us each year this would bring us up to the percentage which in other countries we recognise as frightening and lamentable.

In matters such as this of course a personal assessment is not enough. I have requested and now I request again that a committee of priests, elected by the priests themselves, should be set up now with the task of examining how our life and work and relationships with each other conform to the standards set by the encyclicals and by the Vatican Council.,

I think there is need of it and it should be done as a matter of the greatest urgency.